Urban Flashes Asia

Guest-edited by Nicholas Boyarsky and Peter Lang

AD

Editorial Helen Castle

The greatest achievement of Nicholas Boyarsky and Peter Lang in guest-editing this title of Δ has been bringing to the fore Urban Flashes, an active informal network of practising Asian architects that was founded by Ti-Nan Chi in 1999. This issue does not pertain to be a full account of urban thinking in Asia, but rather an alternative one. As Boyarsky so clearly states in his introductory essay, the predominant modes of considering urban Asia in the West have in recent years been largely confined to corporate practice, which has regarded it as a remarkable commercial opening, and academia, which has perceived it – at arm's length – as a depersonalised 'phenomena'. Thus the immense need to express the almost infinite range of alternatives and diversities within Asian culture that *Urban Flashes Asia* so eloquently signifies but in no way attempts to circumscribe. In his own introductory essay 'Chinatown is Everywhere', Peter Lang further flips these notions aside by presenting urban Asia not as a geographically removed continent but as a constant presence through the Asian communities integrated within all the major towns and cities in the West.

It is, however, the fascination of the Urban Flashes Group with the ephemerality of the Asian city that makes it so impressive in terms of its agility of thought. As Boyarsky points out, this is led by Ti-Nan Chi's notion of micro-tactics, where small-scale interventions become the most potent, and Kazuo Shinohara's 'readiness to learn from the city', which becomes 'a mandate for the architect to act in the city as citizen rather than master planner'. These are all modes of practice that pose strong paradigms for global urban planning and design, as they urge us to look and listen and level ourselves, as city dwellers, before attempting to encroach or impose.

Architectural Design

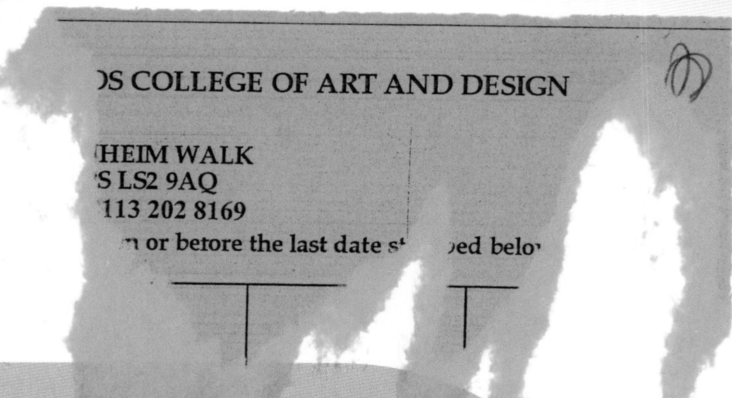

Urban Flashes Asia

New Architecture and Urbanism in Asia

Guest-edited by Nicholas Boyarsky and Peter Lang

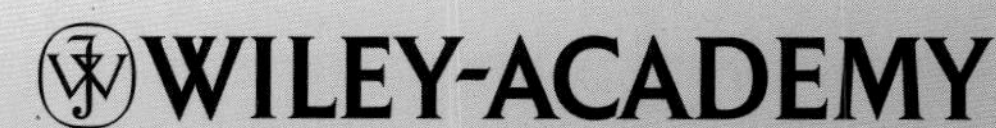
WILEY-ACADEMY

Architectural Design
Vol 73 No 5 September/October 2003

ISBN 0470858311
Profile No 165

Editorial Offices
International House
Ealing Broadway Centre
London W5 5DB
T: +44 (0)20 8326 3800
F: +44 (0)20 8326 3801
E: architecturaldesign@wiley.co.uk

Editor
Helen Castle
Production
Mariangela Palazzi-Williams
Art Director
Christian Küsters → CHK Design
Designer
Scott Bradley → CHK Design
Project Coordinator
Caroline Ellerby
Picture Editor
Famida Rasheed

Advertisement Sales
01243 843272

Contributing Editors
André Chaszar
Craig Kellogg
Jeremy Melvin
Jayne Merkel

Abbreviated positions

t=top, b=bottom, c=centre, l=left, r=right

Front cover: © Ti-Nan Chi

AD
pp 7 & 68-77 © Gutierrez+Portefaix; pp 8-15 © Peter Lang; pp 18 & 21 © Anna Ferrer; p 19 © Heiner Schilling; p 20 © Ti-Nan Chi; pp 22-7 © Karl-Heinz Klopf; pp 28 & 30(tr&c) courtesy Kazuo Shinohara, photos: © Osamu Murai; p 30(tl) courtesy Kazuo Shinohara, photo: © Chuji Hirayama; p 30(b) courtesy Kazuo Shinohara, photo: © Koji Taki; p 31 courtesy Kazuo Shinohara, photo: © Hiroaki Tanaka; pp 32(t), 33 & 34 © Kazuo Shinohara; p 32(b) courtesy Kazuo Shinohara, photo: © Terutaka Hoashi; pp 36(main) & 37 courtesy Kazuo Shinohara, photos: © Tomio Ohashi; p 36(inset) courtesy Kazuo Shinohara, photo: © Japan Architect; pp 38-47 © Team Made in Tokyo; pp 49-53 courtesy Nobuyaki Furuya, photos: © Satoshi Asakawa; pp 54-7 photos: © Sue Barr; pp 60-7 © Gary Chang, EGDE Design Institute Ltd; pp 78-83 photos: © Brian McGrath; pp 84-5 © Bundit Chulasai, Architect, photos: Teerawat Winyarat; pp 86-9 © Ying-Chun Hseih; pp 92-5 © Gwangju Biennale Foundation; pp 96-7 photos: © Justine Graham.

AD+
pp 100-4+ © Kengo Kuma & Associates/Helico, photos: Mitsumasa Fujitsuka; pp 105-6+ © Atelier FCJZ, photos: Cao Yang; p 107+ © Gutierrez+Portefaix; pp 108-110+ © Atelier FCJZ, photos: Fu Xing; p 111+ courtesy Atelier FCJZ, photo: © Liu Yichun; pp 112+ & 116+(r) © FTL; pp 113-5+ © Bentley Systems; p 116+(l) © Buro Happold; pp 117-8+ digital images courtesy of O-Design; p 119+ courtesy Open Office; p 120+(l) courtesy Dia Art Foundation, photo: © Richard Barnes; p 120+(tr) courtesy Dia Art Foundation, photo: Tom Vinetz; p 120+(br) courtesy Dia Art Foundation, photo: Nic Tenwiggenhorn; p 121+ © Albert Vecerka/ESTO; p 123+ © Thomas Deckker 2003; p 125+ © Sandra Ainsley Gallery; pp 126-7+ courtesy ERA Architects Inc. © Cityscape Development Corp.

Published in Great Britain in 2003 by Wiley-Academy, a division of John Wiley & Sons Ltd

Subscription Offices UK
John Wiley & Sons Ltd.
Journals Administration Department
1 Oldlands Way, Bognor Regis
West Sussex, PO22 9SA
T: +44 (0)1243 843272
F: +44 (0)1243 843232
E: cs-journals@wiley.co.uk

Annual Subscription Rates 2003
Institutional Rate: UK £160
Personal Rate: UK £99
Student Rate: UK £70
Institutional Rate: US $240
Personal Rate: US $150
Student Rate: US $105
AD is published bi-monthly.
Prices are for six issues and include postage and handling charges.
Periodicals postage paid at Jamaica, NY 11431. Air freight and mailing in the USA by Publications Expediting Services Inc, 200 Meacham Avenue, Elmont, NY 11003

Single Issues UK: £22.50
Single Issues outside UK: US $45.00
Details of postage and packing charges available on request

Postmaster
Send address changes to AD Publications Expediting Services, 200 Meacham Avenue, Elmont, NY 11003

Printed in Italy. All prices are subject to change without notice. [ISSN: 0003-8504]

Introduction Nicholas Boyarsky

Dirty Cities

In this title of AD, the ever-changing, disorderly or 'dirty' Asian city emerges afresh, redefined from the inside out. Guest-editor Nicholas Boyarsky explains how by airing the pragmatic and perceptive voices of Asian practitioners, Urban Flashes Asia is leaving behind the imposed analysis and globalisation tactics of the West.

Almost all of Tokyo's buildings have been constructed within the last 30 or 40 years, using modern technology. It is this technology that has formed a background to the appearance of shameless spatial compositions and functional combinations, unthinkable in the traditional European city. So what is this city of Tokyo, which can allow such unthinkable productions? How have we managed to arrive at such a different place from that of European modernity despite the availability of the same building technology? ... Shamelessness can become useful, so let us start by considering that these shameless buildings are not collapsible into the concept of 'chaos' but are in fact an intricate reporting of the concrete urban situation.
— Yoshiharu Tsukamoto[1]

'Urban Flashes Asia' charts a paradigm shift in Asian architecture and the city. It gives voice to a unique group of practitioners across a broad range of Asian cities who are actively redefining the Asian environment in their own terms. Western architectural perceptions of Asia have in recent years been monopolised by two contradictory but interdependent factors: the rush of mainstream corporate Western architects to enter a huge emerging market and the rush of avant-garde Dutch architects and theorists to appropriate perceived cultural and environmental difference. These two forms of neo-imperialism, the shamanism of density and the mammon of capital, have successfully rendered Asia both a passive exemplar for innumerable student projects and a willing victim to crass commercial architecture.

Rem Koolhaas's ubiquitous and relentless intellectual drive to normalise and Europeanise, or more succinctly codify so much raw phenomena from new emerging worlds, has been an opportunistic but nonetheless pioneering global enterprise (see, for example, *The Great Leap Forward*[2] for a Koolhaasian judgement on Asian urbanisation, or the recent May 2003 *Wired* 'KoolWorld' for his more recent take on real virtuality).[3] Curiously, his coordinated efforts to understand the entirety of the human physical condition have by consequence succeeded in excluding precisely that which he most hopes to engage and comprehend. Asia is repeatedly cast as a phenomenon, an endless source of inspiration and justification, but it is portrayed without characters, beliefs or cultural identities and traditions.

However, now that the Eurocentric version of Asian has been served up and consumed, there are opportunities to explore behind the scenes and uncover more authentic versions. The glorification of a Western-led globalism is to be welcomed and celebrated for it marks a turning point. As 'Urban Flashes Asia' testifies, local resistances are emerging throughout Asia that challenge Western generalities. Sympathetic and flexible networks are identifying and linking the activities of architects, artists and theorists across the world.

The work shown in 'Urban Flashes Asia' is produced without dogma or reference to Western paradigms. It is pragmatic and concerned with close readings of existing fabric and behavioural patterns; it is informal and preoccupied with self-organising principles. It is individualistic work and, above all, it is highly optimistic. The inevitability of this reaction has been increasingly apparent in recent years and Urban Flashes has become a catalyst that has sparked this chain of self-expression and desire for global connection.

From the Asian side we can see a long-awaited liberation from adherence to the star system of European architectural history whereby lip service must be paid from afar to canons of humanist Modernism. In this issue of *Architectural Design*, when Yoshiharu Tsukamoto speaks of 'shamelessness'; when Kazuo Shinohara speaks of 'the beauty of chaos' and 'progressive anarchy'; when Ti-Nan Chi introduces notions of 'plasm', 'micro-urbanism' and 'tactics'; or when Gary Chang articulates the concept of of 'non-visual pragmatism', we are witnessing the emergence of a new vocabulary and new ordering systems to make sense of the Asian material world. Matter, the ad hoc, appropriation, rapid change and survival tactics – the stuff of Asian cities – become the key other criteria in this developing consciousness. There are here perhaps closer connections to Western anthropological thought, in particular to the work of Mary Douglas on purity, pollution and taboo;[4] to the Surrealists' interest in the primitive and to the 'base materialism' of Georges Bataille than to mainstream architectural traditions.

Considering much of the literature in the field, Bernard Rudofsky's 1965 publication and exhibition 'Architecture without Architects'[5] was a step in the right direction, introducing an alternative world of the 'vernacular, anonymous, spontaneous, indigenous, rural as the case may be'.[6] Other sympathetic Western sources might be found in self-enabling publications from the 1960s, such as *The Whole Earth Catalogue*,[7] which dealt with issues of survival, the concept of tools, self-help and pre-World Wide Web universal accessibility to information.

In the UK, Cedric Price's inspiring work on time, uncertainty and beneficial change developed through projects such as Potteries Thinkbelt, Fun Palace and the Generator.[8] While within the Archigram Group, David Greene's research into the poetic possibilities for technology resulted in pioneering projects such as Botteries.[9] These alternatives, all curiously anarchic or apolitical, form receptive ground for the current Asian condition.

When in this issue Kazuo Shinohara talks of 'a definite division between architecture and the city', he establishes the limits of architecture and at the same time opens architectural discourse to a plethora of new and constantly changing forces that make the Asian city. What may appear at first as a renunciation of control in fact signals a readiness to learn from the city and a mandate for the architect to act in the city as citizen rather than master planner. When Mary Douglas defined dirt as 'matter out of place', she recognised the vital role of disorder in any system: 'Order implies restriction; from all possible materials, a limited selection has been made and from all possible relations a set has been used. So disorder by implication is unlimited, no pattern has been realised in it, but its potential for patterning is indefinite. This is why, though we seek to create order, we do not simply condemn disorder. We recognise that it is destructive to existing patterns; also that it has potentiality. It symbolises both danger and power.'[10] The notion of 'dirty cities' follows from these. The city as a system of disorder is not a city of chaos but one of constantly changing value systems. It is inclusive, fluid and responsive to small actions. Above all, as Peter Lang highlights in 'Chinatown is Everywhere', the dirty city is everywhere.

It is the fascination for the ephemeral, for dirt and for self-organising principles shared by members of

Notes

1 See 'What is Made in Tokyo', p 38 of this issue.
2 Koolhaas states in his introduction: 'A Maelstrom of modernization is destroying everywhere the existing conditions in Asia and everywhere creating a completely new urban substance. The absence, on the one hand, of plausible, universal doctrines and the presence, on the other, of an unprecedented intensity of production have created a unique, wrenching condition: the urban seems to be least understood at the very moment of its apotheosis.' CJ Chung, J Inaba, R Koolhaas, S T Leong (eds) *The Great Leap Forward*, Taschen (Cologne), 2001, pp 27.
3 Rem Koolhaas, guest-editor of *Wired* magazine, 'Koolworld' (on the cover credited as an 'iconoclast'), June 2003.
4 Mary Douglas, *Purity and Danger: An Analysis of Concepts of Pollution and Taboo*, Routledge (London), 2001.
5 Bernard Rudofsky, *Architecture Without Architects: A Short Introduction to Non-Pedigreed Architecture*, MoMA (New York), 1965.
6 Ibid (there are no page numbers in catalogue).
7 For example in Portola Institute, *The Whole Earth Catalogue: Access to Tools*, Menlo, California, 1970.
8 Cedric Price, *Works 2*, Architectural Association (London), 1984.
9 See for example Peter Cook, Warren Chalk, Dennis Crompton, David Greene, Ron Herron and Mike Webb (eds) *Archigram*, Studio Vista (London), 1972.
10 Mary Douglas, op cit.

Opposite
Laurent Gutierrez + Valérie Portefaix, Pearl River Delta, billiards. Now that the Eurocentric version of Asian has been served up and consumed, there are opportunities to explore behind the scenes and uncover more authentic versions.

Urban Flashes that has linked Asian architects with those in the Western world, such as the Italian group Stalker; Casagrande & Rintala in Finland; the Bergen School led by Svein Hatloy in Norway; our own 'Action Research' work and scatter planning typologies; Peter Lang's work on Superstudio and American suburbia; and the work of Austrian architect, film-maker and artist Karl-Heinz Klopf, amongst others. This group continues to grow and respond to Chi's concept of plasmic growth finding reinforcement throughout the world.

Urban Flashes was formed in 1999 by Taiwanese architect Ti-Nan Chi. My first active role in the days leading up to its formation began with a series of spontaneous lectures at the invitation of Chi in Sogo department stores in Taichung, Taiwan, in June 1998. This lightning visit was followed by a series of trips to Asia that defined and expanded a number of urgent issues that would eventually form the core agenda for Urban Flashes, in particular the importance of developing an international network of experimental and highly spontaneous nontraditional working methodologies.

Urban Flashes took its identity through a series of planned actions that Chi was able to orchestrate at the abandoned Hwa-Shan site in central Taipei. In his 1997 exhibition 'Cities on the Move', the Swiss curator Hans Ulrich Obrist had assembled a touring show that combined the work of architects and artists, including Chi himself, from many Asian cities, in response to rapid change and growth. This provided an inspiration for Urban Flashes – the idea that the new Asian city could provide a common ground for discussion across continents.

The first 'Flash' was held in Taipei at the Hwa-Shan site. Participants ('Flashers') from Korea, China, Taiwan, Singapore, Japan, Hong Kong and Europe led workshops of students, engaged the media, lectured about their own work and brainstormed. Situationist tactics were hotly debated alongside the role of technology and environmental concerns. The resulting body of work was influential in the development of the site as a flexible events-led urban park. Last year saw conferences and workshops in Taipei, Linz and London on issues of technology, urbanism and change. Future events are planned for Istanbul and Mexico City.

The future of Urban Flashes will be determined by the sometimes programmed, sometimes haphazard regrouping and expansion of the initial premise, that is, to identify and document, develop and architect a new global platform for encounters within an expanding international community. This non-institutionalised forum will in the future offer many opportunities to share and network information, and process design. ⌂

China-town is every-where

Guest-editor Peter Lang asks why architecture should remain so resistant to cultural interpenetration in a world where there is a Chinatown in every major Western city and no real physical barriers remain between East and West.

> It is a strange city where an apparent disorder and invisible order exist side by side. I concluded that the gap between the absurd mixture of different spaces was what fuelled the vitality of anarchy.[1]

> The undisciplined zones of the metropolis are those in which one can still recognise the possibility of living authentically, building spaces based on a 'local' consciousness that is inseparable either from the experience of participating in daily life (an ongoing dialogue), or from the continuously renewed articulation of the relationship between centres and peripheries, between internal and external, between the known and the (relatively) unknown.[2]

The Wachowski brothers' film *The Matrix*, with two new sequels just this last year, has proven itself to be a worldwide phenomenon with an incredibly broad mass appeal. This apocalyptic digital fantasia, despite its leaden pretentiousness and overcaricatured human society, attempts nonetheless to propel Zen and French philosophies into a swirling mix of heated Hong Kong combat scenes set in stylishly black cowboy Western long-coats. In contrast, it would seem that today's international gurus of architecture barely aspire to erecting a similarly inspired hybridised world of architecture; much less have they considered nurturing the kind of global design philosophy that could successfully pull together East and West into a more kinetic and protean approach to form-making. Curiously, the great weakness of *The Matrix* is its messianic message of loss, a condition of being that is inextricably linked to an overdramatised notion of the sentimentalised decline of civilisations, an all too pervasive vision that is similarly evident in today's architectural culture as well.[3]

The sense of Luddite resistance seems to run deep through continental North American, and large parts of European, society, where speculative home-builders have embraced an agoraphobic simulacra of a 19th-century New England village (Tudor village? Schwarzwald village? Mediterranean village? Take your pick) to satisfy their mass-consumer markets. The visionary prescriptions of today's mainly bicoastal Atlantic architectural avant-garde have become increasingly isolated from global trends by simply failing to deal with these global-scale transformations or to develop appropriately broader critical strategies. Moreover, the major academic institutions and international magazines continue to construct intellectual barriers around themselves, precisely because they continue to defend canonical positions that either discount fundamental transformations in the general architectural culture or proselytise without serious dialectical engagement. Yet judging from the way popular entertainment has taken a leading role in the global spectacle, it is fair to say that audiences are more than willing to contemplate a hybridised heterotopic vision of a future world. And as should be apparent in this issue of *Architectural Design*, there are many voices of diverse provenance that are becoming increasingly engaged in leaping around the boundaries of the architectural canon.

The need to deal with architecture and cities from many different perspectives on a world dimension has never appeared so critically urgent, precisely because without the usual Cold War ideological crutches to sustain the existing system it has only become more difficult to recognise and substitute different links in the

London
Previous spread
Interior display at Victoria Star, Newport Place, Chinatown, London, 2003.

New York
Above left
Kenmare Street, Chinatown, New York City, 2003.

Above right
Elizabeth Street, Chinatown, New York City, 2003.

Opposite
Mott Street, Chinatown, New York City, 2003.

global network. Urban populations have become so squeezed and stretched that the thick social and topographic agglomerations of these cities are virtually unmappable except from satellites surveying from outer space. The unpredictable fluctuations in migrant populations, the ever compressed and frequent cycles of poverty, and the grinding effects of unregulated speculation have for ever altered the established rules of this once aristocratic gentleman's profession. What purpose does an education in architecture have if it refuses to adapt to the revolutionary nature of this generation of emergent urban cultures influencing the way cities behave today? In other words, what is to be done with the lessons learnt among these nondominant cultures that are ipso facto building the future?

Shanghai, Mumbai, Istanbul and Mexico City are the rough-and-tumble urban urchins stealing the limelight on the world stage. The most startling discoveries, important innovations and hotly contested debates are focused here in these great jumbo cities that are energetically renewing their cultural repositories and inventing entirely new urban practices. No academic models today can properly predict the eruptive potential of the 21st-century frontierless city. The legacies of industrial and late-industrial cities throughout Europe and North America are hardly relevant to understanding the sheer complexity of these expanding conurbations spreading across the globe.[4] No comprehensive master-planning can restrain, let alone keep pace with, this late-era phenomenon.

If the obvious circle of Western academics, upholding the dominant canon, is hard pressed to rationalise, and thereby internalise, this cresting urban phenomenon, it will be just as unimaginable to expect earnest contributions in the reconfiguration of a new visionary architecture. The current architectural debate has lost its polemical bite; no architectural thought today speaks passionately for or against another; architecture now is merely a pastiche of trends, rhetorics, technologies, traditions. None of the usual paradigms: the client – corporate or state; the programme – functional or redundant; the style – purist or eclectic, assert any measurable ethic or aesthetic influence on the future course of architecture. One could even argue that there is, in many places, a discernible withdrawal from the debate on the future of architecture altogether, making whatever eclectic association of single disciplines and specialities the default definition for contemporary practice.

There are, of course, many new and pressing issues being brought to the design table, concerning environmentalism, globalism, postcolonialism and the spreading digital information age. However, these risk remaining niche topics within an otherwise overwhelmingly inflexible discourse on architecture.[5] Architecture's long-revered master narrative increasingly finds itself confronting the inadequacy of an academic vision that privileges the neatly structured and closed world-view over the messy assortment of instant ideas and rapid actions coming from so many proximate and distant sources. But the bottom line is that maintaining an elite posture no longer contributes to making desirable commodities for modern survival, nor a truly universal language with which to communicate ideas across ideological divides.

To critically understand the nonfamiliar, one needs to begin by recognising the unpronounceable nature of the subject itself. What then constitutes this other vision, this non-canonic, non-elite, non-Western subject? What term best describes the kind of phenomena we

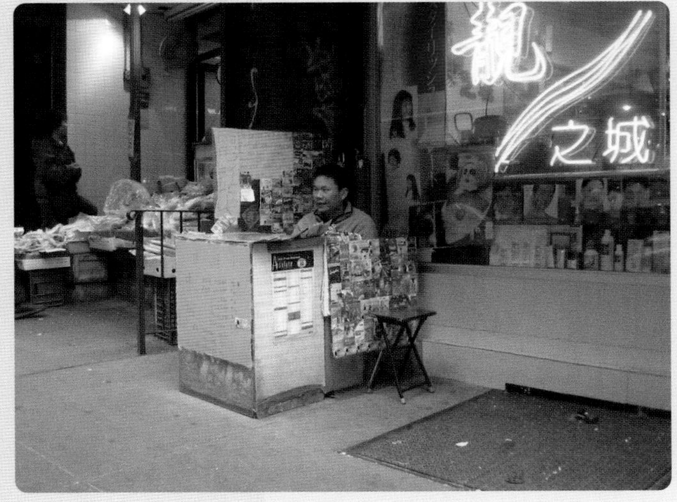

Maintaining an elite posture no longer contributes to making desirable commodities for modern survival, nor a truly universal language with which to communicate ideas across ideological divides.

recognise developing throughout so many regions of the globe but, perhaps particularly in recent times, with so much dynamic force in nations located around the Asian Pacific rim, the so-called 'Asian miracle' cities? Here the greatest perplexity is the result of a confusing mix and mismatch of geographies, cultures, local and global trends. The problem is further compounded by the fact that from the start we have not even a barely adequate way of referring to the Asian phenomenon without borrowing terms from the dominant canon to begin with.[6]

In truth, architects working along the geographical edges of mainstream culture were already for some time aware that the rationalist legacy of the international movement was ill-suited to interpret the spontaneous growth of cities and their corresponding architectural digressions. Architects like Kazuo Shinohara learnt to circumnavigate inflexible dogmas, and instead Shinohara began to build his own perceptive methodology, returning again and again to the chaotic Shibuya district in Tokyo to test the strength of his convictions. Shinohara engages in a critical interplay between canonic and non-canonic models of architecture and city forms to create alternative architecture working methodologies.[7] This and similar kinds of investigation are leading to the documentation of processes, exposing plenty of ready-made localised evidence for entirely new and radical productions in architecture and urban forms.

Franco La Cecla wrote in *Losing Oneself: Man Without Environment*:

> I prefer to speak of 'the local mind' that should be understood as the culture of living, of constructing-living, and not of 'vernacular architecture', 'architecture without architects', 'spontaneous architecture', 'primitive architecture', 'traditional architecture', because every one of these definitions is, not only a humiliation for the immense fresco that is the human faculty for living, but also a definition without hope. It is not the visible remains that give justice to the culture of living. This consists in addition to and moreover of all the visible processes that can be conducted into an edifice.'[8]

It is therefore possible to recognise that the mind's facility to probe and interpret the world is a critical aspect of the act of creation, conditioned on emergent manifestations of local culture in real space and time.

If recognising the changing nature of the subject is the first step in the process of an evolving understanding of architecture, then improvising ways to read these changes becomes essential to the experience itself. In

London
Above
Gerrard Street, Chinatown, London, 2003.

Opposite
Newport Place, Chinatown, London, 2003.

very subtle ways the representation of architecture is changing together with its definitions. The sensually textured photographs of buildings, abstracted to their limpid surfaces and momentarily uninhabited – once popular magazine covers used to seduce a professional public – are increasingly giving way to complex mosaics of images that through their multiplicity link the built world to its living context.[9] The transformation is indeed a function of the changing architectural subject that no longer can be contemplated as an isolated and static moment, but instead requires a dynamic and shifting vision to envelop and wrap the object in its space. These bundled visions of the built environment are not simply part of a temporary trend but represent long-term redefinitions in the engagement and production of space. According to Slavoj Zizek:

> The recourse to Taoism or Buddhism offers a way out of this predicament which definitely works better than the desperate escape into old traditions: instead of trying to cope with the accelerating rhythm of technological progress and social changes, one should rather renounce the very endeavor to retain control over what goes on, rejecting it as the expression of the modern logic of domination – one should, instead, 'let oneself go', drift along, while retaining an inner distance and indifference towards the mad dance of this accelerated process, a distance based on the insight that all this social and technological upheaval is ultimately just a non-substantial proliferation of semblances which do not really concern the innermost kernel of our being.[10]

Zizek considers these oriental-inspired antidotes to Modernism as symptomatic of today's peculiar cultural burden. But his statement also recognises that the specific condition has forced the marooning of society from its spiritual centres, revealing the symbolic depressions pocketing today's contemporary technologically driven global culture. Entire populations float within these drifts, leaving ample evidence that the artefacts of daily life have been undergoing serious transformations as well. But one of the more curious long-term effects is the increasing mixing of traditionally distinct cultural worlds, the blending of East and West, the commingling of identities even when deliberately and xenophobically resisted.

A vast spectrum of universal daily-life activities and by-products are now interchangeably transferred from one end of the globe to the other. 'Gameboys', animated cartoons, nanotechnologies and pet robots are but some of the ubiquitous signs of commonplace cultural

Notes

1 See Hiro Hemmi, 'Anarchy and Beyond: An Interview with Kazuo Shinohara', in this issue.

2 Gianni Vattimo, 'Preface', in La Cecla, *L'uomo senza ambiente*, Bari, Laterza (Rome), 1988, p xi.

3 Clearly this experience of loss behind the West's perceived decline requires more discussion than space permits here, especially as digital technology seems only to have accelerated the general sense of alienation. For a start, see Joseph Rykwert's investigation into 'Adam's House', where he conjectures that much architectural theory is based on this primal concern. He states: 'The return to origins is a constant of human development and in this matter architecture conforms to all other human activities. The primitive hut – the home of the first man – is therefore no incidental concern of theorists, no casual ingredient of myth or ritual. Much of today's contemporary popular cinema remains fixated with apocalyptic futures that tend to degenerative myths; popular

Paris
Above
Terrace, Les Olimpiades, Paris, 2003.

Right
Entrance to shopping mall, Les Olimpiades, Paris, 2003.

Berlin
Opposite
Vietnamese Market, Meeraner Strasse, Berlin, 2003.

architecture is following in a similar path.' J Rykwert, *On Adam's House in Paradise: the Idea of the Primitive Hut in Architecture History*, MoMA (New York), 1972, p 192.
4 Contemporary North American and European cities have been quietly expanding into their suburbs and peripheries, but these really locally indigenous patterns are only gradually receiving sufficient attention among the elite institutions still largely fixated with centre city issues.
5 Green architecture, for example, does make a lot of sense already and will surely succeed in addressing concerns for the world's shrinking resources, but architects, planners and landscape architects are not about to effect major changes until a significant shift takes place within the population at large – not that impossible to imagine if one thinks about the advances achieved in other similarly contested areas of the body politic. But as long as the most pollutant nations on the planet shirk environmental responsibilities, green architecture will remain experimentally challenging but only minimally relevant: hopefully the 'green' movement will not become a mere sidebar to Western academic politics as usual.
6 The descriptive minefield that we face when attempting to define 'Western' and 'non-Western' or when identifying precisely Asian from Central Asian, Near Asian or Southeast Asian, is another issue altogether. I would like to acknowledge a series of conversations on this subject with Esra Akcan for her help in setting out this condition. Akcan teaches critical theories on world architecture at Columbia University. She is currently working on her PhD thesis provisionally titled 'Modernity in Translation: German-Turkish Exchanges in Land Settlement and Residential Culture'.
7 See Hiro Hemmi, 'Anarchy and Beyond: An Interview with Kazuo Shinohara', in this issue.
8 La Cecla, op cit, p 5.
9 Architectural publications have been changing dramatically since Rem Koolhaas's and Bruce Mau's *SMXL* appeared some ten years ago.
10 Slavoj Zizek, *On Belief*, Routledge (London), 2001, pp 12–13.
11 See Edward Said's *Orientalism*, Vintage Books (New York), 1979, for deeper insight into this contested world of representations and misrepresentations.

penetrations that call into question Western cultural hegemony in the first place. In other words, there really are no barriers, frontiers or limits separating Western and non-Western cultures but merely degrees of interpenetration. Take, for example, the extraordinary number of communities rising distant from native sources, such as the 'Chinatowns' in New York, London, Berlin and Paris. The frequency of exchanges, the multitude of interrelations, all conspire to erode the principal notion of exclusivity, racial identity, cultural uniqueness and legacy.

We should still heed the warnings, however, that recognise the shortcomings of an over-romanticised, clearly nonhistorical vision of the Orient conveniently serving as a depository for a large part of the world's uncategorised exotica.[11] A stagnant view of the East effectively eliminates contemporary working strategies that could possibly question or even subvert existing Western hegemonic tendencies. In any case, the networks of communications, transportation and economic investments already tie vast swaths of the East to the West, reinforcing the observation that Chinatown is indeed everywhere. Yet it is precisely this progressive entanglement of living cultures weaving back and forth across continents that makes the task of building a non-canonic architecture all the more obvious: Chinatown is not really an ethnic demarcation; it is really a designation for a means to a different end, as can be observed in the way Chinatowns have adapted, mutated and influenced the myriad cities on every continent where they have been taking root.

The promise offered in the collection of articles in this issue of *Architectural Design* is one of reconciliation and dialogue between East and West precisely because there are plenty of indications that many observers from both have already opened themselves to the kind of cross-fertilisation that makes this type of exchange uniquely creative and rich in potential. Stepping outside the dominant canon is necessary because the hegemonic narrative acts to suffocate emergent tendencies whether from distant lands or from nearby landfills. Two-way dialogue has the potential to expose and spread new cultural experiments, crossing and crisscrossing increasingly obsolete ideological barriers. The goal is to work with a multiplicity of master narratives: to understand the way architecture fits together with the world, not how the world can be forced to fit to architecture. 'Urban Flashes' offers several such snapshots, prescriptions for an already existing future world. Δ

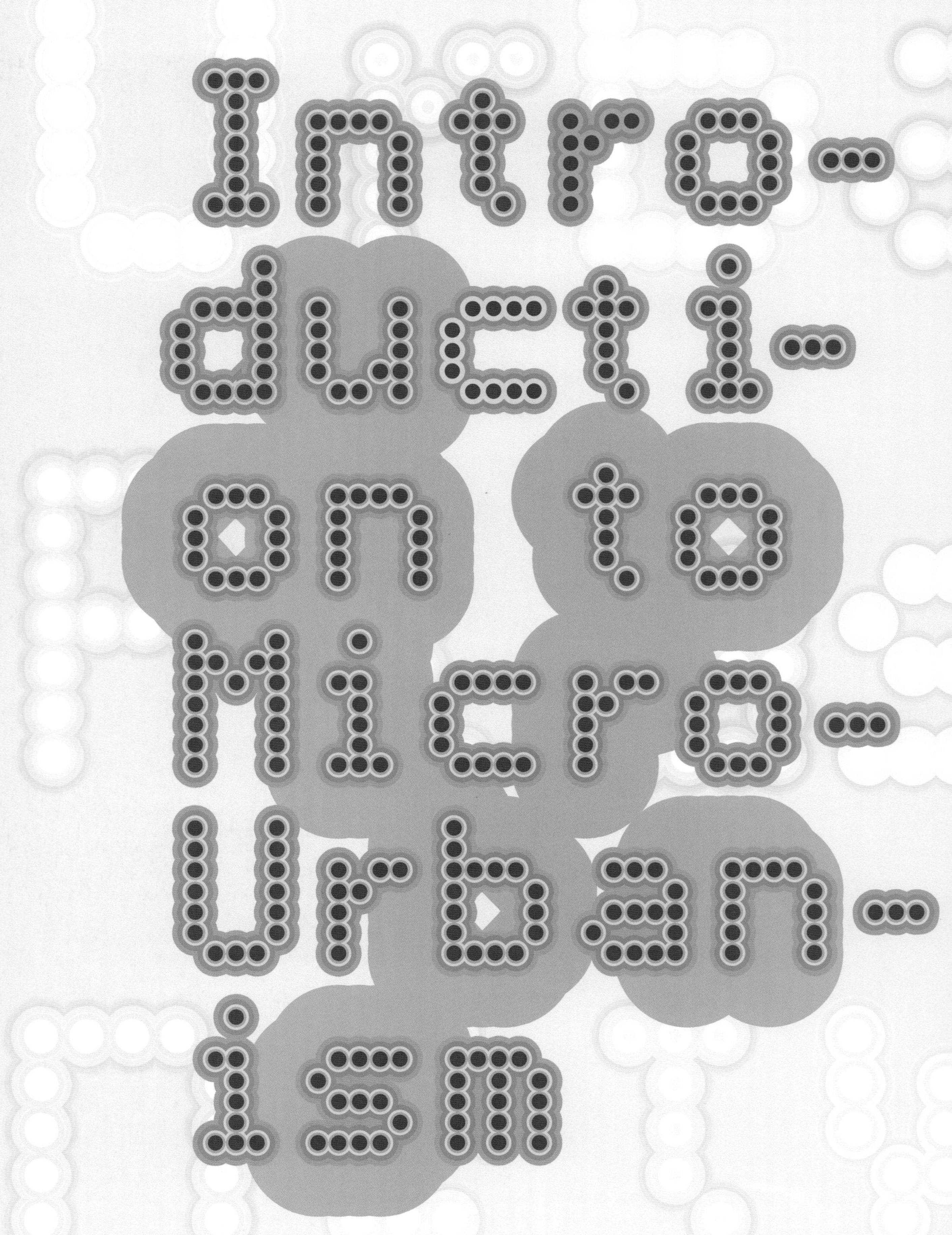
Intro-
ducti-
on to
Micro-
Urban-
ism

As hard-headed ideological, large-scale urban interventions are no longer relevant or even desirable, new tactics have to be forged to interact with the present urban condition. Here, the founder of the Urban Flashes network, Ti-Nan Chi, advocates effective tactics on the micro-scale. He explains how micro-urbanism or in-between actions might be used to directly enrich the living environment.

War is the father of all things and the king over all.
— Heraclitus, 500 BC

In my speech, 'Thinking the Unthinkable', for the opening of 'Cities on the Move' at Secession in Vienna, 1997, I treated the expanding high-density development fuelled by advanced technology in a new generation of booming mega-cities as the signal for a historically unprecedented urban condition capable of drawing the attention of the art and architecture vanguard. I suggested a way of thinking that went beyond the existing planning methods today. Karl-Heinz Klopf, an artist based in Vienna whom I met in 1995, was especially impressed by the dazzling effect of lights and projection of spaces in Tokyo. We have been working together under the banner of Urban Flashes ever since.

The first 'Urban Flashes' workshop was realised in 1999 in Taipei, when15 architects and artists from Europe and Asia were invited to work on strategies to revitalise the use of the abandoned sites in the Hwa-Shan area for art and cultural purposes, via proposals for encouraging public awareness and the process of negotiation with the city's formal institutional sectors. The results of the workshop were widely publicised and later triggered the development of the Hwa-Shan area into a visionary urban park in conjunction with information technology, a project that is now being officially implemented.

The events of 11 September 2001 only reinforced our motivation and deepened our conviction that a new global condition was upon us, clearly underlying the urgency to locate new forms of architecture and city planning. In 2002, three consecutive Urban Flashes events were held in the form of symposiums in Taipei, Linz and London, and the Urban Flashes network of architects and artists gradually evolved into a collective force similar to an alternative NGO.

The ideas being stated in this text do not necessarily represent Urban Flashes as a group. However, they were inspired by the 'Flashers' (participating architects and artists of Urban Flashes) and our transient meetings. Nonetheless, though they share the same mindset, all of the Flashers have their own unique approach. Since the formation of the group, we have become more and more aware of our role in the formation of the future city, which is neither a heroic demonstration nor grass-roots resistance as we know it today. Rather, we are forging in-between actions with micro-scale tactics to generate a better living environment.

Today the city contains patchworks of different physical characteristics and social-cultural situations. The presupposed congeniality has already been lost, even in old-core urban areas. The public can find much at fault with years of careless planning, yet at the same time no one is quite sure how to check this vicious circle that promotes the hasty agglomeration of masses and volumes that continues the blind pursuit of prosperity.

To examine the city from a macro-scale level is no longer effective when current chaotic phenomena are often illegible, and even more misleading under more formal analysis. We have seen efforts to invent or resurrect dominant structures, to demonstrate heroic rectifications, to reinforce the regulations and so on, in order to battle with the so-called urban 'disease'.

Micro-urbanism suggests there are internal realities to be investigated in order to describe how things interact and coordinate in the micro-scale realm that manifests the true spirit of a city and its people. The inner reality comprises not only repetitive, robotic activities but also a plasma of conflicts and actions. People survive not within a rational state but in this more plasmodial mode of living, as our observations generally have revealed.

Plasm

Inside cities, where countless ongoing exchanges and clashes take place, we experience daily incidents together with our own private struggles – some that can be identified as forms of war, and others that are forms of interaction and negotiation. Such phenomena can be described as plasm, to indicate the primal state of living that has long been ignored and misinterpreted in architecture and city planning.

The multinucleate cities in Asia manifest this dispersed situation of mutations and complexities. The hidden side beneath the visible forms in fact occupies the bulk of the public realm, which is bewildered by the irrational fluctuation of emotions and actions. In entering the public domain, in-situ interactions function as art that goes beyond set rules and modes of negotiation. The unstable and chaotic flows of encounters and engagements exemplify the bursting energy in the city that excites human behaviour and building activity.

Right
Transformation of the European city. A residential block in Barcelona is demolished revealing temporary traces of its construction. The development was a politicised act that provoked neighbourhood protests and police response.

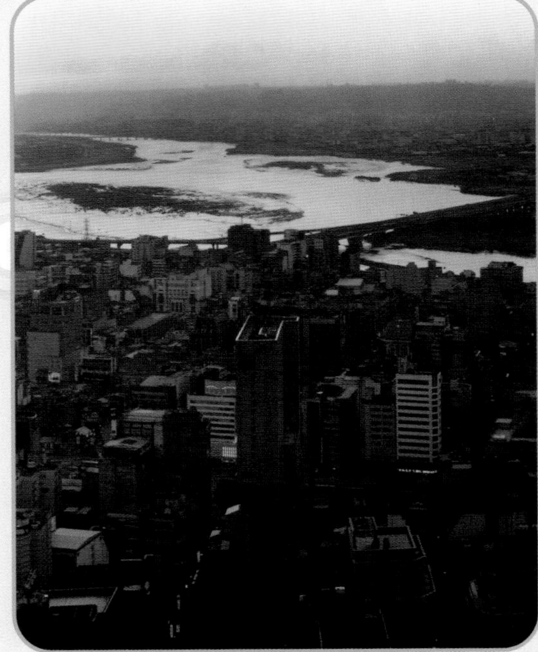

Our instant encounters now have even more fluctuations with the universal use of mobile telecommunications. Following rapid market demands and immediate-response capital investments, cable lines, antennae and halfway stations, often without integrated planning or without permit, are installed above or below the city's existing buildings. These attached transmitting accessories do not usually follow the conventional infrastructure but spread in the direction of the transmitter's broadcast patterns. As nodal links to individuals and other coexisting worlds, they change the cityscape and divert activities in the city from within and afar.

The fear of increasing density is contingent on the mounting pressures over scarcer resources and insecurity regarding the exploitative nature of society. Density as a quantitative problem may be resolved by distribution and disposition. But there are unavoidable congestions that arouse a sense of uncertainty. Congestion is more critical and often more a psychic issue than a pragmatic problem. To accommodate vast numbers of residents we need to agglomerate masses and volumes to produce another landscape that offers new combinations of wonder and excitement. Technological progress, however, does not necessarily facilitate life's many bewilderments. Neither do growing levels of transit mobility and speed capacity provide any more freedom and safety. An individual is easily overwhelmed by consumeristic techno-fever. Floating signs and information billboards have built a new dimension that tumefies our conscious and forms of dominance. For those living in the cities, the need to be mobile simply means the possibility of improving circulation, an ability to adapt to countless restrictions, and the chance to escape surveillance.

The plasmodium, or slime mould, is a primitive life-form commonly found in forest ecosystems. When unfavourable conditions occur, the plasmodium changes from an animal-like multinucleate protoplasm to the appearance of a fungus, thus well adapted to its surroundings via migration or a renewing life cycle.

The plasmodium reflects the content of our clammy urban living. People survive by utilising technology and limited resources, and by maintaining an interdependent and intramural proto-organic relationship.

Architecture and city planning were once surgical exercises that were little suited to diagnosing urban internal micro-scale problems, while building activities are assumed to be regulated and controlled by pragmatic operations. The formalistic urban structure of a sanitary building project excludes the latent tumorigenic factor from its formula. Meanwhile, the neoplasm-like illegal constructions and settlements are vital and spread quickly across cities, evidence of how the residue is transformed into inseparable and indispensable parts of the larger city.

In many ways similar to plasmodia, people tend to migrate into new territories to begin a new life. When the given living condition is bad, or when the condition gets worse, people manage to recycle their limited possessions and reinvent their cocoons. The convertibility and self-help nature of the local community has become a forgotten factor inside the preconceived ready-made society; worse, it has been gradually discarded as the remnants of anarchic criminality.

The notorious nomads of the city, the homeless, might not be without homes. Rather they are taking a pathway leading to the reconstitution of their lives. Wandering peddlers move around the streets with simple personal effects committed to their carts and the routes. In reality, this can be read as a form of eco-wise behaviour humans conduct in order to survive in the harsh urban environment.

Abandoned industrial sites, private and public vacant buildings, and city peripheries are the empty areas of a city, places that provide refuges and alternatives for people who need rooms within which to breathe and roam. The areas of urban emptiness signify the darker side of master-planning and grand-scale development but somehow, even within these environments, there is room for beginning anew. Worse yet would be to fill these voids using singular-minded planning methods that merely cage the potential urban vitality.

Tactics

> Thus the highest realization of warfare is to forge strategies; next is to deal with alliances; next to charge the armed forces; and the lowest is to attack their fortified cities when unavoidable.
> — Sun Tze, *Art of War*, 500 BC

War awakens the need to understand confrontations. Today we observe hectic conflicts and fighting on the

Above
Aerial view of Taipei revealing the city's bursting energies that are generated by the unstable and chaotic flows of encounters and engagements.

streets as well as through the media. People are constantly seen making strategic moves to gain advantage or to escape from danger. Modern planning, however, does not take account of daily activities that are often marked by the degree of uncontrollable human will. Instead, planners use grandiose hypotheses to sanction these inevitable ongoing actions.

These in-situ moves, which support fundamental survival tactics in everyday life, need to be recognised and examined. They are themselves the core of social-political dynamics that induce change within cities. The following are major tactics derived from observations on the more obscure aspects of daily life as the point of departure for micro-design and planning.

Vacuity

> Subtle! Subtle! It approaches the formless.
> — Sun Tze, *Art of War*, 500 BC

Taoist metaphysics attends to the world's needs of the weak and other intangible behaviours. Less is not only considered to be more, but more critical, no matter how vulnerable it appears to be. In line with Tao–Zen thinking, minimalists have worked on the purification of the preconceived form to obtain a spiritually abundant state. However, this concern with aestheticisation has never reached the heart of the transient and formless side of being.

Non-Euclidean geometry and digital fluid systems are now being employed to accommodate entire facets of the ever-changing context in the hope of introducing the vitality of the free spirit. In fact, forms and shapes themselves do not necessarily bear transitory meaning. It is the overall setting that allows for the interplay with the formal and the formless which influences people's deep comprehension and judgement.

The Tao Art of War emphasises the subtle play of intangible substance to formulate strategic deployments. The formless or transient substance can be utilised in either a visible or invisible manner. And the ultimate strength depends on the total effect of the arrangement in time and space. Except for the placement of masses and volumes, architects have to magnify the limited resources at hand, usually with small or insignificant elements, to create preferred conditions that help things to flow.

Topos

> Configuration of terrain is the prerequisite to warfare. Judging the given conditions, taking control of victory, estimating ravines and defiles, the distant and near, is the Tao of the commanding.
> — Sun Tze, *Art of War*, 500 BC

The ground we are attached to raises the innate awareness of our existence, which is invisible but nonetheless incomprehensible. Alteration of the grounding plane results in the mobilisation of senses and perceptions. The topos constructs our horizons, and conditions our biological mechanisms and physical activities on earth.

Paul Virilio's suggestion of the oblique circulation was an attempt to gear towards this fundamental revolt. The installation of Tangibleintangible was a case, on a very manageable scale of operation, of how people and goats walk on slightly slanted or sloped ground to further unveil the insignificant determinant in the space.

The techniques of bridging and dis-bridging are both crucial in building up the strategies for access to such significant manoeuvres. The efficiency of these strategies includes the speed of construction or destruction and the understanding of the sloping river banks to be connected or disconnected.

To occupy a strategic location in a city devoted to seeing and being seen should become a priority for working in the field. Selection of location can be based on the knowledge of the topography, scenery and psychogeography of the area, which offers insight to choose the relationship to the surroundings in order to ignite positive engagements and prevent fatal entrapments.

Deception

> Thus although capable, display incapability to them. When committed to employing your forces, feign inactivity. When it is nearby, make it appear as if distant; when far away, create the illusion of being nearby. Attack where they are unexpected. Go forth where they will not be expected.
> — Sun Tze, *Art of War*, 500 BC

Appearance is understood as the direct contact with perceivers. Instantly, this produces the impression of the substance behind the surface. To shape a preferred look, it is almost unavoidable to apply camouflage or mount illusion. The deceptive approach is not just a psychological wrestling but also aims for an understanding of the existing reality, aiming to find a channel for formal engagement.

Betel nut is the seed of a tropical palm-tree flower common in Southeast Asia, and has a stimulant effect

Above
Ti-Nan Chi, Tangibleintangible installation, IT Park, Taipei, 1998. The installation asks people to consider the sort of impact of a slight shift in terrain on both our senses and physical movements. Goats and people are forced to walk on slanted ground in a limited area.

Opposite, bottom
Santa Marta, Colombia. The plasm and plasmodium of urban living conditions. Dwellings and landscape merge into a primal stage, which evokes the true process of urban development.

when chewed. In Taipei, the young girls who sell such nuts are referred to as 'Betel Nut Beauties'. Dressed in sexy costumes, they stand inside or outside a flashy glass booth to entice those driving by to stop and buy betel nuts. The lavish bodies and settings are designed for interaction, therefore to be constructive parts of the city.

At the same time, illegal vendors need to be able to disappear when chased by the police. Their carts, containers and sheets are therefore designed to be movable, dispersible and restorable. The retreat is planned in advance. These time-conscious apparatuses are effectively inserting into intervals of dullness and commandment.

Detour

> If they are substantial, prepare for them; if they are strong, avoid them. If they are angry, perturb them; be deferential to foster their arrogance. If they are rested, force them to exert themselves. If they are united, cause them to be separated.
> — Sun Tze, *Art of War*, 500 BC

To survive in a highly dense and competitive environment, one has to take the risk of being on the fringes of norm and danger. In order to play safe, sometimes one needs to subvert the dangerous zone. This detour could be seen on the collective level practised long before the emergence of Situationist ideas regarding *détournement*.

In Bangkok, street vendors gather along the sides of the railway tracks, forming the city's daily food market. When trains come, the vendors remove their goods and sheds behind the track. When trains go, the marketplace is reassembled. In Taipei, taxi drivers cut into a line of moving vehicles to get out of a jam or to speed up. Using radio phones, those who share the same interest may gather on certain sections of the road to protest or to unite in pressure on the police or an opposing group of taxi drivers. They are turning the road into an action arena coexisting with the civilian use for transportation.

Bunker

> And a correspondence dawned on me as between these places of shelter from danger, and places of worship, which are also places of salvation.
> — Paul Virilio, *From Modernism to Hypermodernism and Beyond*, 1997[1]

The third stage of speed revolution, as Paul Virilio pointed out, suggests that we are now more than ever living in a reduced, bunkerised space. With the aid of digital technology, cyber travel provides an autistic virtual womb from which dwellers can be reborn. On the other hand, people see the city as a battlefield and are always seeking their bunkers. A bunker is not necessarily a monolithic fortification. The bunker can be found spaces and temporary structures when its location is strategically near points of observation and access to the supply – like true stories of warriors spread over the vicinity. Though the facade of an idyllic house may remain, underground cellars and tunnels become the living room for retreating troops.

Architectonic traces of the above-mentioned tactics have in fact existed since the beginning of time, and can be found in any city on the globe. When strolling in Brussels we see gradually evolving colonnades and steps connecting walkways to different levels of routes and open spaces, which is in itself a micro-urban device. Using the background of this city as a conceptual demonstration, I propose using a 4-metre 3-D grid as a general reference to allocate small elements that accommodate activities and structures. The small elements will be given qualities similar to nanomaterials to enable the instigation and reorganisation of the urban fabric via a smart disposition of these micro-urban elements. The mechanism is expected to contain free connections, multiple interactions, autonomous divisions, individualistic bunkers and propagandable masses.

In deploying these tactical elements inside the existing urban landscape, the city is stripped naked and reveals exigent political actions and exchanges in the public sphere. This is also about how we like to treat the history of a city that has never been merely one-faceted. The folded corners and liminal areas need to be uncovered and penetrated in order to expose the process through which the city constantly updates its equilibrium. 4

Note
1 John Armitage (ed), 'From Modernism to Hypermodernism and beyond: An interview with Paul Virilio', *Paul Virilio: From Modernism to Hypermodernism and Beyond* (London, Thousand Oaks, CA, and New Delhi: Sage), 2000, p 32.

Way of

Display

Urban Tactics in the Context of the Betel Nut Culture in Taiwan

In Taiwan, the commercialisation of the sale of betel nuts – a mild stimulant when chewed – has spawned the development of an entirely new makeshift building type, the betel nut stall. These temporary stores or simple mobile units, staffed by 'Betel Nut Beauties' who dress up to lure their customers, have cropped up all over the country. The Austrian artist and film maker **Karl-Heinz Klopf**, who is currently working on the digital feature film *By Way of Display*, which explores this subject, describes the major impact of the betel nut culture on Taiwanese urban life.

Previous spread
Betel Nut Beauties dressed in 'uniforms' to attract customers.

The informal sector
Above
Containers and betel nut booth.

The Informal Sector

Booming economic growth-spurts as well as recessions develop new urban spaces and new forms of life and survival in accordance with their respective cultural contexts.In Taiwan, a society which lives predominantly in cities, a new space- and work-provision branch, often subsumed in the informal sector, has emerged as a result of the extremely fast economic development of the second half of the last century and the necessity to manage this state of affairs.

During this period, existing buildings were illegally expanded in all directions, a situation that was tolerated due to the need for increased production and storage space. Living rooms suddenly became factories, and the 'family as a factory' became a promotion slogan. Mobile makeshift constructions emerged for the selling of everything possible.

Probably the most culturally interesting and particular sector is that which has developed out of the new marketing strategies for betel nuts – a new, independent culture, created by various regional and global influences.

Planting–Selling–Chewing

According to the most recent studies, the chewing of betel nuts can be traced back thousands of years to mountain tribes in the southwestern part of the island. In the 17th century the first wave of the Han came from southern China, and it was they who adopted and continued this tradition. Today the cultivation of betel palms, which often takes place illegally, especially in the mountains, and the subsequent marketing of betel nuts, is a national economic factor.

Top
Pull-out betel nut booth.

Bottom
Betel nut booth under construction. The box can be moved, on bars, back to the arcade.

Betel nuts are consumed predominantly by long-distance truck drivers and males in the lower economic classes, who each consume as many as dozens a day. The effect of chewing is a feeling of warmth in the body caused by the stimulation of the central nervous system, acting as an aphrodisiac and also mildly intoxicating. However, it is also claimed that regular consumption can lead to oral cancer.

The cultivation of betel nut palms and the marketing and consumption of the nuts have now found their way on to the streets of Taiwan. Throughout the country there are roughly 100,000 'booths' selling betel nuts, and these are most commonly found along highly frequented roads, crossings and highway turn-offs.

From a distance, truck drivers can identify these booths by their peacock signs made from colourful fluorescent tubes, and by their often large number of flashing lights. The signs overpower the confusing density of billboards and advertisements concealing the building facades, and this illumination of the street spaces increases as one gets closer and closer to the betel nut booths. Floor-to-ceiling shop windows, rollable glass boxes or containers on stilts, all painted in happy colours, are supplied with cut-out glass surfaces and mirrors offering a spatial structure for young girls wearing tightly fitted 'uniforms' – the so-called 'Betel Nut Beauties' (Chinese *binlang hsishi*).

If one pulls up in front of one of the booths, a Betel Nut Beauty swiftly steps out to your vehicle to take your order. Betel nuts, cigarettes, energy drinks, information about the area and, if it is not too busy, a brief chat are all on offer. It is this service, the conspicuous appearance of the girls combined with the possibility of

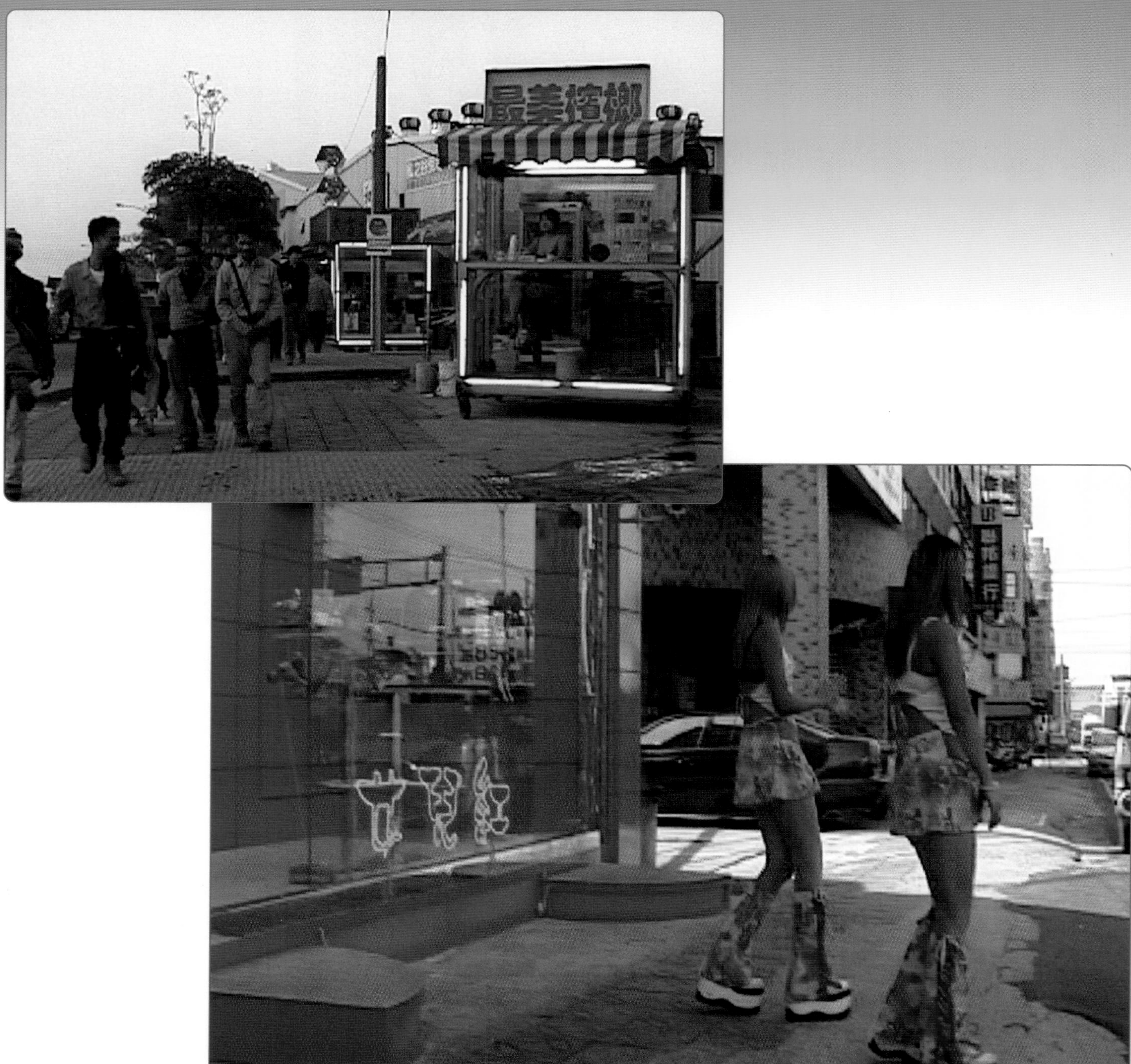

Everyday life of the betel nut business

Top
Betel nut booths designed as glass boxes on wheels.

Bottom
Orange betel nut shop and 'beauties' in matching 'uniforms'.

having a short interaction of closeness during the otherwise dreary workaday world, which is the most essential aspect of success in the bitterly contested betel nut market.

Performing the Streets

With the swift expansion of the highways, brought about by the construction work in the cities and the resulting massive increase of commercial traffic in the booming 1970s and 1980s, the habit of chewing betel nuts quickly spread throughout all regions of the country and also within the cities. At the same time came the growth of the informal sector, in the form of illegal expansions and extensions to existing buildings, in order to cover the rapidly increasing need for space. The streets were marked by temporary stores, simple mobile units, and the early betel nut stands were no different.

However, the great pressure of competition around the middle of the 1990s forced many betel nut vendors to develop new marketing strategies, and tactics for attracting clients became increasingly sophisticated. With the use of colourful, flashing lights and scantily clad girls a lively display was designed to seduce the senses on otherwise rather unattractive streets. The girls change their 'costumes' every day – nurse, military, school uniform or characters taken from Japanese Manga stories are just some of the themes that are alternately presented to the motorised clients. Taipei-based architect and Urban Flashes initiator Ti-nan Chi sees this as deceptive appearances, as a kind of tactic on a micro-urban level that urban planners and designers can learn from.

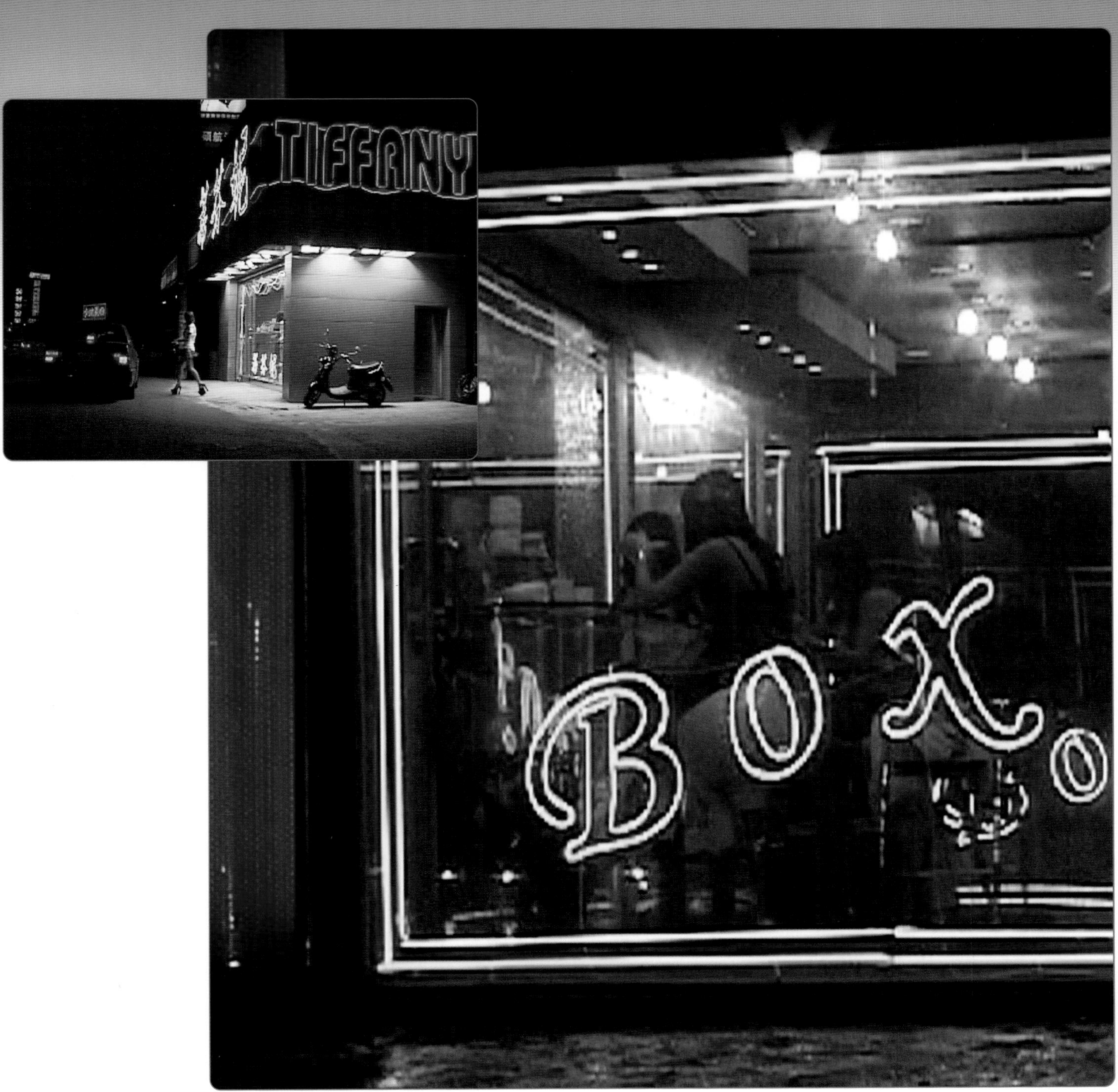

Betel nut shops at night
Above, main image
Last-generation transparent betel nut shops designed with Western names.

Above, inset
Betel nut shop 'Tiffany'. The young owners carefully design their new stores giving their products a better image to win new customers from the middle classes.

The potential of the street as a space for performing is here explored in a highly delicate way. Sometimes the girls will stray out into the traffic, waving and using dance-like movements to make their presence known, giving them a sense that they are the stars of the streets. This self-impression of out-of-the-ordinary is supported and displayed in these colourful productions by incorporating ingredients of the pop culture: flashing lights, loud pop or techno music and spicy costumes. Though such offensive strategies generate higher profits, they also very often result in hefty fines and sometimes traffic accidents.

It is hardly surprising, then, that the owners of these betel nut businesses have developed increasingly ingenious systems of disappearing. One example of this is the vending box on bars, which can be pushed from the pavement into an existing building within a minute. And other booths can easily be loaded on to a truck and set up for business elsewhere.

However, apart from the other negative effects of the betel nut business, for example land erosion through illegal cultivation, mainly in mountain regions, or the possible damage to health, this phenomenon is an example of dynamic and creative spatial intervention, which has, without planning, quasi-anonymously arisen in an in-between area of official structures. Here we are dealing with a cultural form that develops out of its own traditions, current conditions and foreign influences, where thousands of stands along the busy streets have created an authentic service network over the entire island, the potential of which can provide other possibilities for communal and cultural development. ᗡ

Anarchy and Beyond

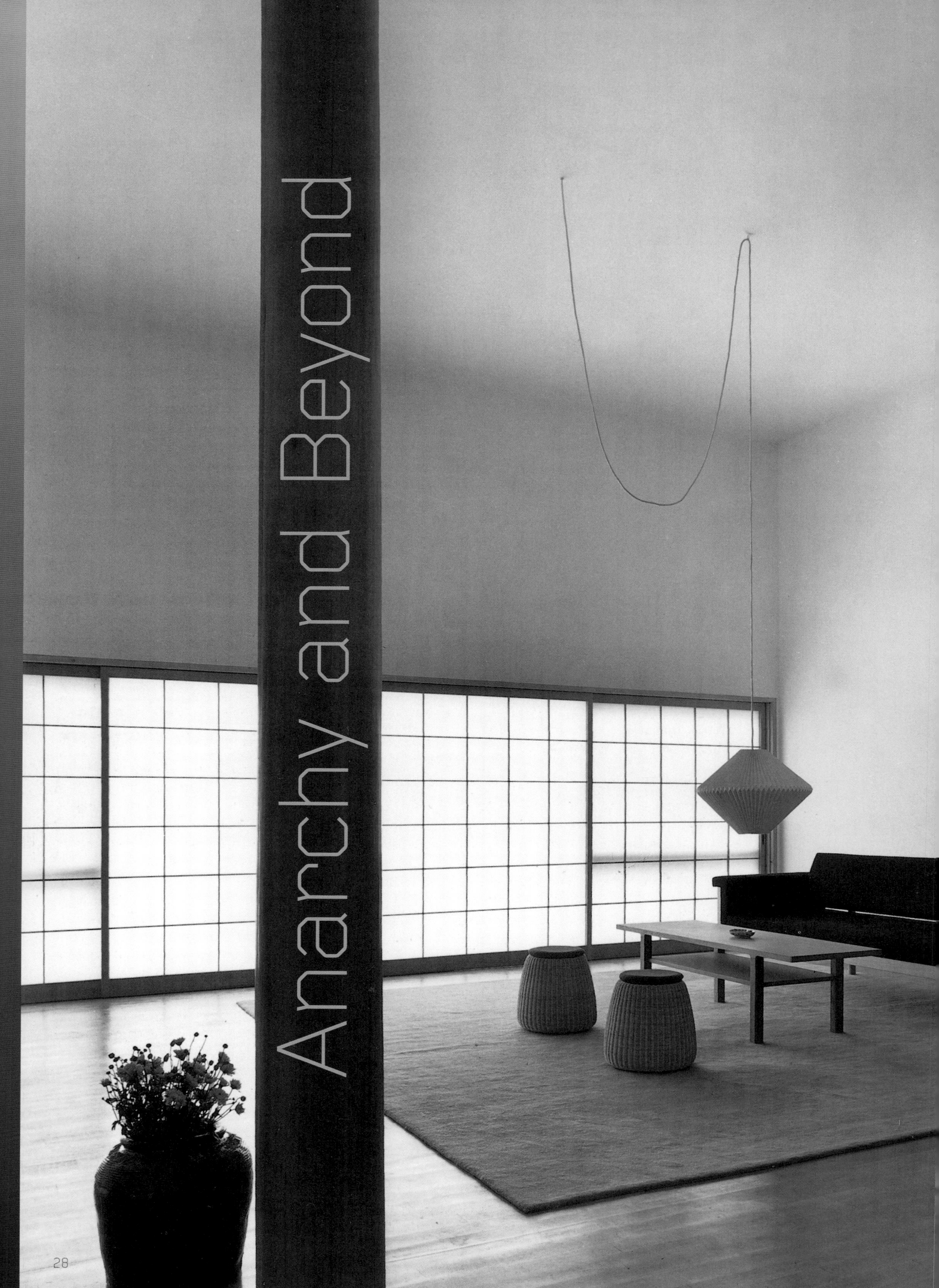

An Interview with Kazuo Shinohara

Kazuo Shinohara has been one of the most influential architects in Japan. The 'Shinohara School', a label dubbed by architectural magazines for architects who have either studied with Shinohara or have been influenced by him, now encompasses an impressive array of leading Japanese architects. The minimal yet provocative houses for which he is widely known are an obvious source of this influence. Equally influential but not as widely available outside Japan, are his manifestos on architecture and cities. Here, **Hirohisa Hemmi** interviews Shinohara on the development of his urban thinking and ideas.

> 'In the mid 1960s, I introduced the concept "beauty of chaos" to explain the situation in Tokyo. I used this concept of chaos in a positive context, not only in architecture but as a logic for understanding the world.'

Shinohara may have been the first architect to recognise chaos as a positive and an essential element in a contemporary city. Although the terminology echoes the 'chaos logic' in mathematics, a field which he abandoned in the early 1950s, his concept was in no way a reference to the 'chaos theory' in mathematics which was established in the mid-1970s. Although his idea of chaos resonated with the cutting edge of scientific research, it was 'intuitive' and highly personal, 'coming from a very strong self-confirmation on why the visual disorder of Shibuya area where I passed every day was not unpleasant'.

Inherent in these words is his basic stance, to gain understanding through reasoning within the parameters of architecture and not through reference or analogies. It is a method similar to a mathematical process of demonstrating a theorem and it can be traced to his unique beginning as an architect. 'As a researcher in mathematics, I went to Kyoto around 1950 for a conference. There I was overcome by a strong feeling towards traditional Japanese architecture and decided to pursue a career in architecture. From the bipolarity of the two disciplines, I attained the true antithetical, ambivalent way of thinking. I felt intuitively that if I were to immerse myself in the strong attachment towards traditional architecture, nothing new would emerge. So I consciously tried to confront tradition through logic. Although my affection towards tradition has not changed, I have used negation as a method to take the process of creation to the next stage.

'In the 1950s, when my strong affection for traditional architecture led me to pursue a career in architecture, the pioneers of modern Japanese architecture were absorbing Modernism via the US, using the Katsura Villa as a point of reference. A mere coincidence that Katsura Villa and compositions of Mies van der Rohe looked similar proved pivotal in the acceptance and spreading of Modernism in the 1950s. I, on the contrary, felt that the Japanese tradition was fundamentally different from the tradition of Mies or from the column and beam structures of Le Corbusier, and focused on this point, elaborating and clarifying the differences in my PhD thesis "Research in the Spatial Composition of Japanese Architecture". What seems similar in appearance is in actuality the opposite, was one of the conclusions.

'The architectural movement that began from an interest in a particular aspect of Japan and Europe, which was similar by coincidence, was successful for a while but never acquired the energy to endure. The pioneers connected traditions of Europe and Japan without much reason. They couldn't see beyond the similarities to notice the differences.'

Opposite
House in White, Tokyo, 1964.

Opposite, top left
Kugayama House, Tokyo, 1954.

Opposite top right
Uncompleted House, Tokyo, 1970.

Opposite, middle
Umbrella House, Tokyo, 1961.

Opposite, bottom
Tanikawa Residence, Kita-karuizawa, 1974.

Above
House in Higashi-Tamagawa, Tokyo, 1973.

The Logic of Ambivalence

'Logic of ambivalence refers to my method of allowing contrasting meanings to define my existence simultaneously,' says Shinohara. This idea is central to his approach to architecture and becomes apparent when one traces the transitions in his architectural works, which are grouped into what he calls 'styles', according to shared themes.

'In the First Style where Japanese tradition was the central theme, I was in search of objective approaches to confront Japanese tradition while being conscious of my strong affinity towards its expression. After the completion of my first work, House in Kugayama,[1] this approach became a conscious method of composition. I then focused on a small contrast within Japanese tradition, that of the residences for the noble class, as exemplified by Katsura Villa, and that of the common people, namely the farmers, and designed House with Earthen Floor and Umbrella House, which shared qualities with rural dwellings. In the designs to follow, I placed another filter and arrived at House in White, which cannot be categorised into either of the two strains of residential architecture.

'If my First Style can be summarised in these words, the Japanese, abstract, cubic space realised in House in White became the genesis for the theme in the Second Style. Here, I pursued the possibility of contemporary Japanese expression distinct from a literal expression or familiarity with Japanese tradition. From the Uncompleted House I would consciously generate counterpoints and contrasts to embark on my exploration of what I called the "cube". I realised in my pursuits that although it was possible to share affinities with the geometric cubes of European Modernism, expression of richer qualities inherent in the cubes of the Middle East or North Africa could not be achieved. This realisation led me to the Third Style, which explored compositions liberated from both Japanese tradition and the cube of European Modernism.

'In the design of Tanikawa Residence, located in the mountain resort of Kita-Karuizawa, which is known for its lush greenery and abundant rain, wooden structure and sloped roofs were logical points of departure. I used these elements as a prerequisite and attempted to differentiate this house from the houses of the First Style. From around this period I began dialogues and confrontations with the previous two styles already completed. It is a very complex process of negation, in no way related to the straightforward negation of Modernism by those who embraced Postmodernism. Being fully aware of the attachment to the things I had designed and positioning a new composition in contrast, they were attempts to see where this process would take me. In the Second Style, for instance, it was an attempt to

Top
Shibuya at night, 1979.

Bottom
Exterior view. House in Uehara, Tokyo, 1976.

see what can be designed to counter the flowing, gentle slopes and the eaves of traditional structures. In the Third Style it was a dialogue with the First Style in one instance and with the Second Style in another. A typical example of this process is the House in Uehara. It began as a complete cube into which a structural system of column and braces, a highly personalised system with connections with the Japanese tradition, is juxtaposed.'

A brief overview of Shinohara's first three styles reveals the complex play of opposites at many different levels of his house designs, which he considered as a concentrated expression of architecture. At a much broader scale of opposites, he addressed the issue of the city and houses or architecture in general. Here, it is important to emphasise that the city and houses were considered opposites and not seen as elements in a continuum. At the foundation of his ideas on cities is his notion of the city 'as an entity completely independent of houses'.

Citing that Modernists in Japan often made reference to Le Corbusier's Voison Plan to claim house and city as synonymous, and that the concept for houses could be applied directly to cities, he declared this idea invalid and that 'houses could represent only as far as architecture in general but not the city'. He considered architecture as a result of a creative will but saw the city as an ever-changing mathematical system comprised of an innumerable number of determinants. By placing a definite division between architecture and the city, he diminished the role of the architect as the creator of cities, thus allowing for a more objective and critical observation of cities.

Beauty of Chaos

Shinohara's concept of 'beauty of chaos' came about as a response to the emergence of a new genre called 'city design' in Japan in the 1960s. Some architects of his generation claimed that house designs that did not

address city design issues were defective. This view, shared by the majority of architects at the time, was based on the assumption that cities could be planned. Shinohara, on the other hand, claimed that 'if each architect spoke on cities freely, there would be as many ideal cities as there were architects, and as long as this situation was not resolved, city design was not logically possible nor worth trusting'.

'To dismiss city design only by this reasoning is correct and I think it is still valid today. That is precisely why we have cities like Tokyo, which for me is not misguided but rather is the only possible outcome. Nothing else can logically exist. The social condition, personal possessions, the configuration of the land survived through generations – these factors alone can make Modernist coherence in cities unachievable.'

Apparent chaotic state in cities was inevitable as well as charming for Shinohara. So, in the climate of optimistic megastructure being proposed to replace the 'ugly' existing structures of Tokyo, he stated emphatically that this 'charming' chaos 'should not be seen as the object of criticism nor demolition'.

Progressive Anarchy

As the visual chaos of the area around him proliferated throughout the 1970s, Shinohara introduced the concept 'progressive anarchy' to explain this new condition in the city. In a manifesto entitled 'Toward Architecture', he identifies 'beauty of chaos' as vitality or energy one feels when walking in areas such as Shibuya, and continues on his exploration to uncover its essence.

'I recognised that the vitality of the city was borne out of the conviction that each and every building was the most sleek and beautiful. I observed that while the most up-to-date electronics technology filled the streets there were also rows of small wooden houses just behind, the strictly ordered interiors of which suggest the persistence of such formalised aesthetics, with roots in the Middle Ages, as that of flower arrangement and the tea ceremony, though in fragments. It is a strange city where an apparent disorder and invisible order exist side by side. I concluded that the gaps among the absurd mixture of different spaces were what fuelled the vitality of anarchy.'

From around this time, the area around Shibuya station began to gain the attention of many architects from abroad. Shinohara says: 'What attracted these jet-setting architects could not have been exoticism. I think it was the beauty or the vitality, appealing to the emotions which celebrate life that is quite different from the aesthetics of Europe.'

This phenomenon, along with Tokyo becoming recognised as one of the most exciting cities in the world in the 1980s, was welcomed by Shinohara as a demonstration of his idea of 'beauty of chaos' in actuality.

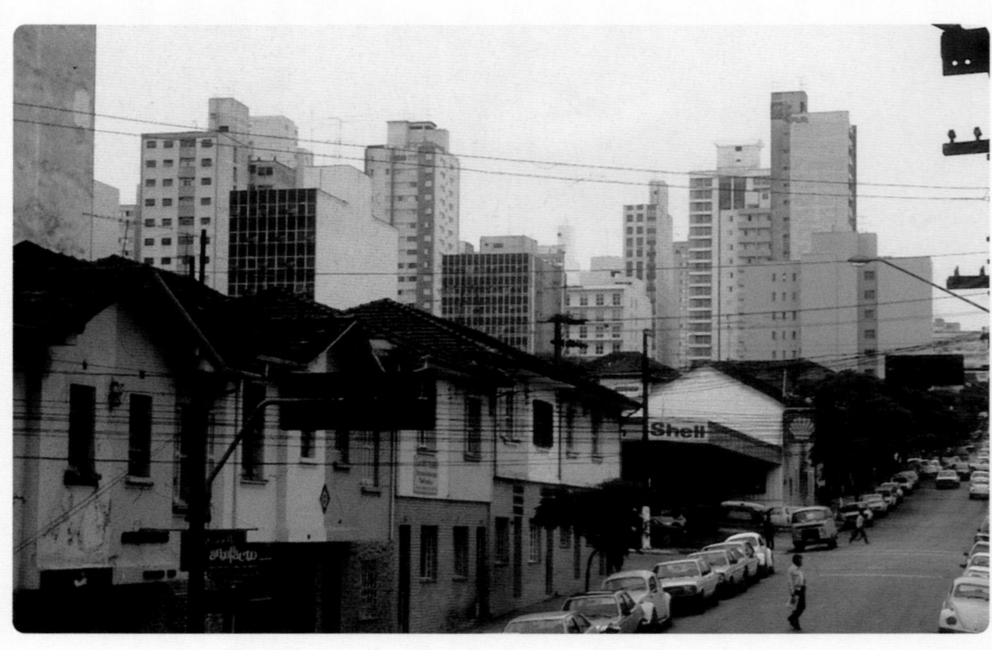

Top
Hachiko Plaza, Shibuya, 1979.

Middle top
Shinohara's evaluation of chaos in cities as a positive quallity does not repudiate the silent quarters of a city where time seems to stand still; they are equally important qualities in his concept of cities. (Left to right): Ouagadougou, Burkina Faso; Bisac, outside Cuzco, Peru; Cuzco, Peru; Fez, Morocco.

Middle bottom (detail)
Order and disorder in Tokyo.

Right
Order and disorder in São Paulo.

Super-Big Numbers Set City

In 1999, Shinohara introduced the concept 'Super-Big Numbers Set City', which was derived from yet further changes occurring in the area around Shibuya.

'At around the time the concept "Progressive Anarchy" was introduced, the area around Shibuya station became the centre of youth fashion. Towards the end of the 1990s, many venture businesses of information technology were drawn to the area and the name "Bitter Valley",[2] dubbed after "Silicone Valley", became popular. The area is synonymous with cutting edge and people gather intuitively with the expectation of finding something interesting. This connection with the younger generation created new energy which was transformed into innovative developments in the IT sector. Chaos is often associated with poverty or with an approaching catastrophe, but the visual chaos seen around Shibuya is of a totally different kind with no association to such negative factors. It has vitality all its own.

Shinohara's unique approach involved a continuous observation of a particular phenomenon in Tokyo over time to derive a series of concepts. He would then test their validity against the phenomenon of Tokyo as a whole. It has so far proved effective in uncovering an essential quality of Tokyo.

'As in the recent situation in Tokyo, if the hardware and software which make up this phenomenon become very large in number, the character of the "big number" itself begins to determine the outcome. This is what I call "Super-Big Numbers Set City". Here, the power of an individual becomes negligible. Whatever is done architecturally will not bring about any change to the city itself. It's not accurate to say that architecture will be engulfed in such a city but that it becomes elements to enhance the vitality of the whole. Even if one were to make a large building, the city will not be transformed by its emergence.'

Anarchy and Beyond

Shinohara's unique approach involved a continuous observation of a particular phenomenon in Tokyo over time to derive a series of concepts. He would then test their validity against the phenomenon of Tokyo as a whole. It has so far proved effective in uncovering an essential quality of Tokyo. Although his manifestations are limited to Tokyo, he has recently undertaken a project with his former students to observe cities outside Japan using his theories and concepts[3] to test their validity. He has made some preliminary observations and is now in the process of searching for a concept model for further exploration.'

Shinohara sees future cities all over the world coming to resemble Tokyo. He cautions, however, that eradication of the existing buildings to replace them with the 'Tokyo' model would be disastrous.

'Take Shibuya, for example, they could have made the condition in 1979 a preservation zone. That corner pharmacy was quite something. I think the vital issue is how the world deals with this dynamic from now on, because if the whole world became a homogeneous "big number", it would be unbearably boring. So when I talk of the next issue, it refers to how we can formulate a new mechanism which can effectively confront the "big numbers" at a global scale.

'I have maintained that "chaos" as seen in Tokyo is a positive quality, from the concept of "beauty of chaos" to "super-big numbers set city". However, this does not preclude my stating that the quiet scenery I encountered in cities in such areas as Peru or Morocco, where time seems to be absorbed into space, is also worthy of note. Appreciation of "chaos" must not mean repudiation of Peru or any other situation. Without the other, the world cannot exist.'

From this stance, Shinohara arrives at the idea of 'world cities'. It is not yet fully defined but is comprised of two opposing images at the foundation of his notion of cities, namely quarters where silence is predominant and streets full of hustle and bustle. He sees the 'world city' as a city in which the two images 'function side by side, without losing their respective definitions'. It is a city that reflects his basic stance of ambivalence, relative certainty of the existing set off against the new to allow for constant rejuvenation.

Shinohara's current project is to formulate ways to make this concept valid while designing a house to correspond to it. It is a creation of a minimal space to correspond to the vast world – back to the process likened by Jean Nouvel to a scientific experiment of 'introducing small amounts of foreign organism to see its effect on the larger whole'.[4] Shinohara goes back to the design of houses because he believes that 'just as neutrino is involved in the birth of the universe, the smallest of spaces can logically go face to face with the vast world'.

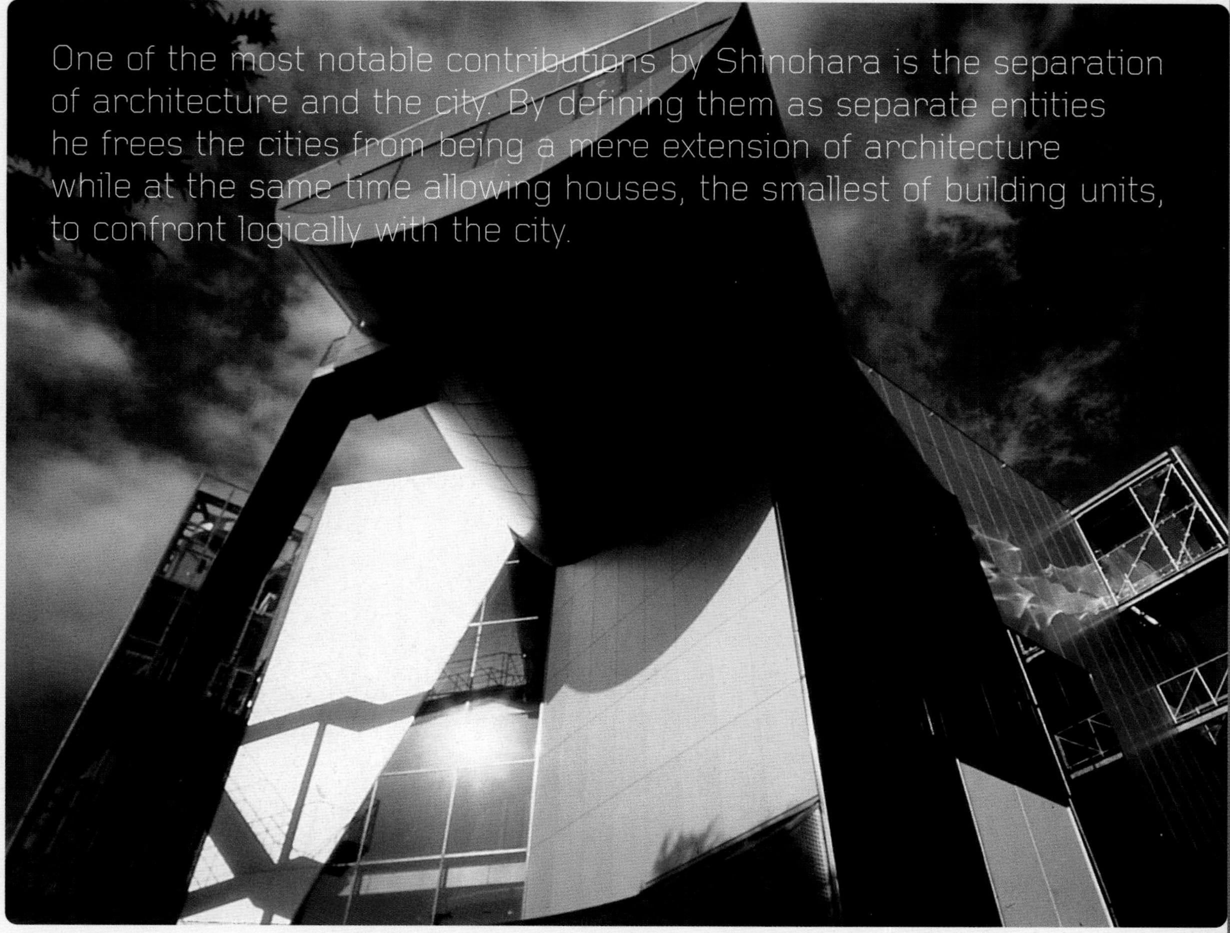
One of the most notable contributions by Shinohara is the separation of architecture and the city. By defining them as separate entities he frees the cities from being a mere extension of architecture while at the same time allowing houses, the smallest of building units, to confront logically with the city.

Postscript: Opposites as the Essence

During the interview, Shinohara makes reference to Le Corbusier's Voison Plan as epitomising the limitations of Modernist logic. However, it should be pointed out that his evaluation of Le Corbusier is not at all negative. In an informal conversation following the interview, Shinohara identifies Le Corbusier's ambivalence as a key quality. He credits this quality as vital in making Ville Radieuse valid; and says that without Ronchamp, which emerged as an expression of his nonrational side, his rational side would not have endured. But he goes on to add that Le Corbusier was not able to include these aspects into his logic. Shinohara's attitude is that of ambivalence, and Le Corbusier's theories are incorporated into his creative process of negation.

This attitude towards Le Corbusier is demonstrated in his 1979 paper entitled 'Towards Architecture'. The title is no coincidence and he draws on the Tomcat fighter plane and the lunar module to explain his ideas, just as ocean liners and biplanes were used as analogies in Le Corbusier's version. He is quick to add, however, that his is not so much a visual analogy as a demonstration that the Tomcat's true capabilities and functions are not directly reflected in its outward appearance.

Shinohara's architectural exploration is devoted to formulating a logic to reconcile sets of opposites such as logic/emotion and rational/nonrational. In other words, he takes on the project the Modernists had embarked on and explores it further by expanding the boundaries of its logic to transcend its much criticised exclusivity. The interview reveals the 'logic of ambivalence' as central to his thought process throughout his career. Not only his houses but also his theories on cities, which have not been as widely publicised outside Japan, share the same structure. He recognises the gap between opposites as a source of vitality in cities and introduces the concept of 'world cities' as a means of resisting the trend to be uniformly chaotic. At first glance it may seem conflicting for an architect to proclaim chaos as a positive quality and then to also warn against its uniform dissemination, but it is entirely consistent in the logic of ambivalence since reconciliation of opposites lies at its very essence. In this way, Shinohara carefully defies the inclination to converge, to keep his logic open and inclusive.

One of the most notable contributions by Shinohara is the separation of architecture and the city. By defining them as separate entities, that is to say, architecture as a result of a process of creation, and the city as a result of their agglomeration, he frees the cities from being a mere extension of architecture while at the same time allowing houses, the smallest of building units, to confront logically with the city. Countless examples of planned cities gone astray seem to support this distinction. Yet the strongest support seems to come from the body of work he has produced based on this premise. Although ironic, the works he created through a complex system of negation, self-reference and differentiation begin to resemble a real city with a sense of vitality surpassing that of any planned city. AD

Notes

1 This house was seen to evoke the feeling of Katsura Villa as pointed out by a reviewer for *Architectural Review* magazine. (AD April, 1958).
2 Shibuya is written as a combination of Chinese characters which mean 'bitter' and 'valley'.
3 The observations were compiled in a book entitled *Discourse on Tokyo from Tokyo via Kazuo Shinohara*, Kajima Publishing (Tokyo), 2001.
4 Dialogue between Shinohara and J Nouvel, '"Ultimate Modernism" to change architecture?', *Kenchikugijutu*, January 1988.

Opposite (main)
House under High-Voltage Lines, Tokyo, 1981.

Opposite (inset)
House in Ashitaka, Ashitaka, 1977.

Above
Tokyo Institute of Technology, Centennial Hall, Tokyo, 1987

What
Made in

is
Tokyo?

Japanese magazines and textbooks formulate an idealised and tasteful view of architecture that is ultimately unobtainable in such a densely populated city as Tokyo. The actual reality of the urban situation is that it is occupied by 'disgusting' new buildings of shameless spatial compositions and functional combinations. Transport links, housing and leisure facilities often overlap in a single building or in uncomfortably close proximity. Here, **Yoshiharu Tsukamoto** (with co-authors Momoyo Kaijima and Junzo Kuroda) suggests that rather than turning their heads away from the 'shamelessness' of this architecture, architects should be learning to look to it as a 'reporting of the intricate urban condition'.

The Appearance and Disappearance of Shamelessness

When returning to Tokyo, especially from Europe, I'm often surprised. Roads and train lines run over buildings, expressways wind themselves over rivers, cars can drive up ramps to the roof top of a six-storey building, the huge volume of a golf practice-net billows over a tiny residential district. Major European cities are still using the buildings of previous centuries, and have not been modernised in terms of building stock renewal. By comparison, almost all of Tokyo's buildings have been constructed within the last 30 or 40 years, using modern technology. It is this technology that has formed a background to the appearance of shameless spatial compositions and functional combinations, unthinkable in the traditional European city.

So what is this city of Tokyo, which can allow such unthinkable productions? How have we managed to arrive at such a different place from that of European modernity despite the availability of the same building technology?

Changing Our Surroundings into Resources

Today, architectural magazines and university textbooks are filled with famous works, East and West, old and new. Specialists such as practitioners and critics find their criteria by looking at overseas examples and Japanese classics, but though this is correct and necessary the values woven by this situation reveal Tokyo as a city covered by disgusting buildings. If our footsteps are actually embedded in a pitiful urban landscape, the idea of using famous architecture as a criteria base seems just an attempt to express good taste. Photographic books amplify a desire for an architecture that simply cannot be found in our surroundings.

If it comes to this, then suddenly architectural design no longer holds any interest; the future of such work appears depressing. However, the reality of Tokyo is that it is already fully occupied by such 'disgusting' buildings. If we cannot attempt to turn these into resources, then there is no particular reason to stay in this city. Surely we can begin to think about how to take advantage of them, rather than running away. Shamelessness can become useful, so let us start by considering that these shameless buildings are not collapsible into the concept of 'chaos' but are in fact an intricate reporting of the concrete urban situation.

Survey Beginnings

In 1991 we discovered a narrow spaghetti shop wrenched into the space under a baseball batting-centre hanging from a steep incline. While neither a spaghetti shop nor a batting centre are unusual in Tokyo, the packaging of the two together cannot be explained rationally. Despite an apparent convenience in their unity, it is not necessary to hit baseballs towards the opposite hotel, sweat, and then eat at a spaghetti shop. In addition, it is difficult to judge whether this is an amusement machine or a strange architecture. The building simultaneously invited a feeling of suspicion that it was pure nonsense, and expectation in its joyful and wilful energy. But we also felt how 'very Tokyo' were the buildings that accompanied this ambiguous feeling. Having been struck by how interesting they are, we set out to photograph them, just as though we were visiting a foreign city for the first time. This was the beginning of 'Made in Tokyo', a survey of the city's strange and nameless buildings.

Da-me Architecture

The buildings we were attracted to were those giving priority to stubborn honesty in response to their surroundings and programmatic requirements without insisting on architectural aesthetic and form. We decided to call these 'da-me architecture' (no-good architecture), with all our love and disdain. Most of them are anonymous buildings, not beautiful, and not accepted in architectural culture to date. In fact, they represent the form of building that has been regarded as exactly what

Previous spread
Made in Tokyo Map – Da-me Architecture
'The buildings we were attracted to were those giving priority to stubborn honesty in response to their surroundings and programmatic requirements without insisting on architectural aesthetic and form. We decided to call these "da-me architecture" (no-good architecture), with all our love and disdain. Most of them are anonymous buildings, not beautiful, and not accepted in architectural culture to date.' But if you look closely 'in terms of observing the reality of Tokyo through building form, they seem to us to be better than anything designed by architects. These buildings are not explained by the city of Tokyo, but they do explain what Tokyo is.'

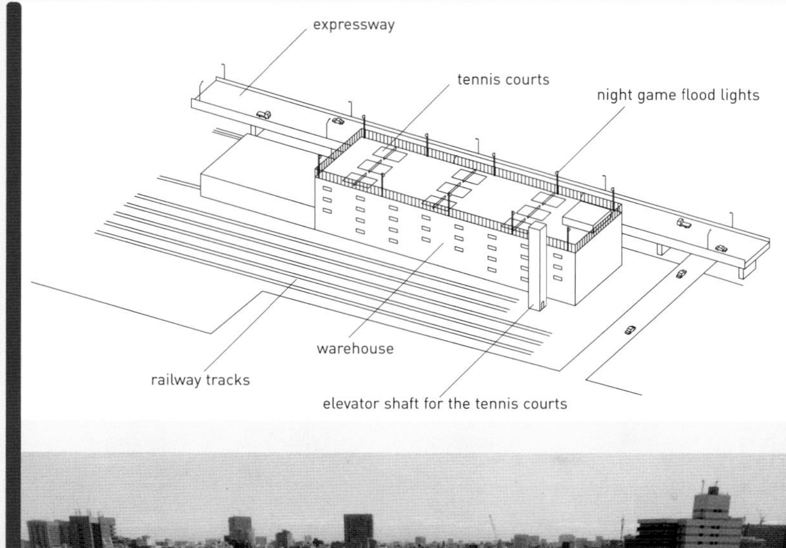

Tokyology, and the spatial expression of architectural works displayed confusing urban landscape as a metaphor; our goal was to get away from the attitude that the city can be summarised by metaphorical expression. From the start we avoided considering examples that could be read as stereotypical images, for example stylistic eclecticism and contrast between pre- and super-modern. We decided to try to avoid working with nostalgia.

The examples we stuck with were based more on particularity in the way they related directly to use. By treating the relations between elements as the major issue, we tried to see the object without preconditioned meanings and categories. We tried to look at everything flatly, by eliminating the divisions between high and low cultures, beauty and ugliness, good and bad, a way of seeing we believed was called for by the urban space of Tokyo – a gigantic agglomeration of an endless variety of physical structures.

There are too many exceptions to be able to convincingly deduce each building's composition from the urban structure. So if we try to collapse da-me architecture into a typology, we will lose the interesting mongrel nature of the differing elements. Our flatness means something more specific.

Above
Warehouse court
Function: Warehouse and tennis court
Site: Iidabashi, Chiyoda-ku
On the second floor of the Iidamachi goods-train station and paper-dispatch centre is a platform for the delivery of paper around the country; the third to fifth floors are dedicated to the store of paper and the first floor is the truck yard for dispatching. Almost the entire floor area of the train station and dispatch yard's roof space, 160 metres by 50 metres, is used as tennis courts. The courts can be accessed directly by an elevator shaft which stands independently of the main volume of the building. Lighting facilities for night games also light up an advertisement – the tennis school looking for students.

architecture should not become. However, if you look closely there is just one strong point to them. In terms of observing the reality of Tokyo through building form, they seem to us to be better than anything designed by architects.

These buildings are not explained by the city of Tokyo, but they do explain what Tokyo is. So, by collecting and aligning them we believed that the nature of Tokyo's urban space could become apparent. Although at the time a best-selling guidebook to Tokyo was full of architect-designed works, it did not show the bare Tokyo we had experienced. It could not answer the question of what kind of potentials lay in the place in which we were standing. What can it mean to think about and design architecture beside da-me architecture?

Flatness

The starting hypothesis for the survey is that the situation and value system of any city should be directly reflected through unique buildings. In the case of Tokyo we suspected that in da-me architecture could be found the key to understanding the city and its architecture. However, the definition of da-me architecture was not necessarily clear from the beginning. We debated at length over each example as we collected them, taking care not to think about the city as a conceptual model. In the 1980s a background of chaos affirmed theory and

Guidebook

The result of the observation also depends on the method of representation. If the method doesn't suit the observation, the result often cannot be grasped. It is therefore important to develop a method of representation that does not lose observational quality. The format we chose here was that of a guidebook. Tokyo is a giant maze-like city without physical navigational aids such as axes or urban boundaries, and it is perhaps for this reason that there are innumerable guidebooks on every facet of life in this city. Tokyo has already been edited to suit every possible objective. Even if they form a kind of software after the fact, in terms of organising the way the city is used, guidebooks can become a tool for urban planning. However, a guidebook does not require a conclusion, clear beginning or order. This seems suitable for Tokyo, where the scene is of never-ending construction and destruction.

From Architecture towards Building

The buildings of Made in Tokyo are not beautiful. They are not perfect examples of architectural planning. They are not A-grade cultural building-types such as libraries and museums. They are B-grade building-types such as car parks, batting centres or hybrid containers including architectural and civil engineering works. They are not 'pieces' designed by famous architects. However, what is nonetheless respectable about these buildings is that they do not have a speck of fat. What is important right now is constructed in a practical manner by the possible elements of that

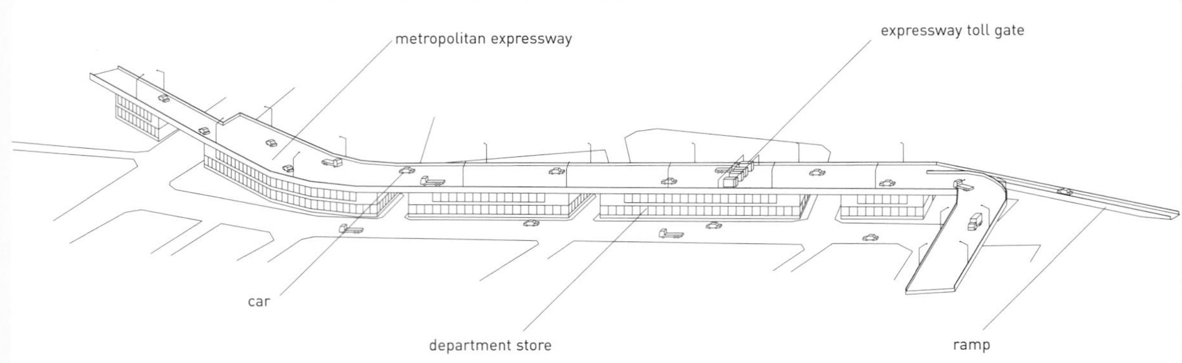

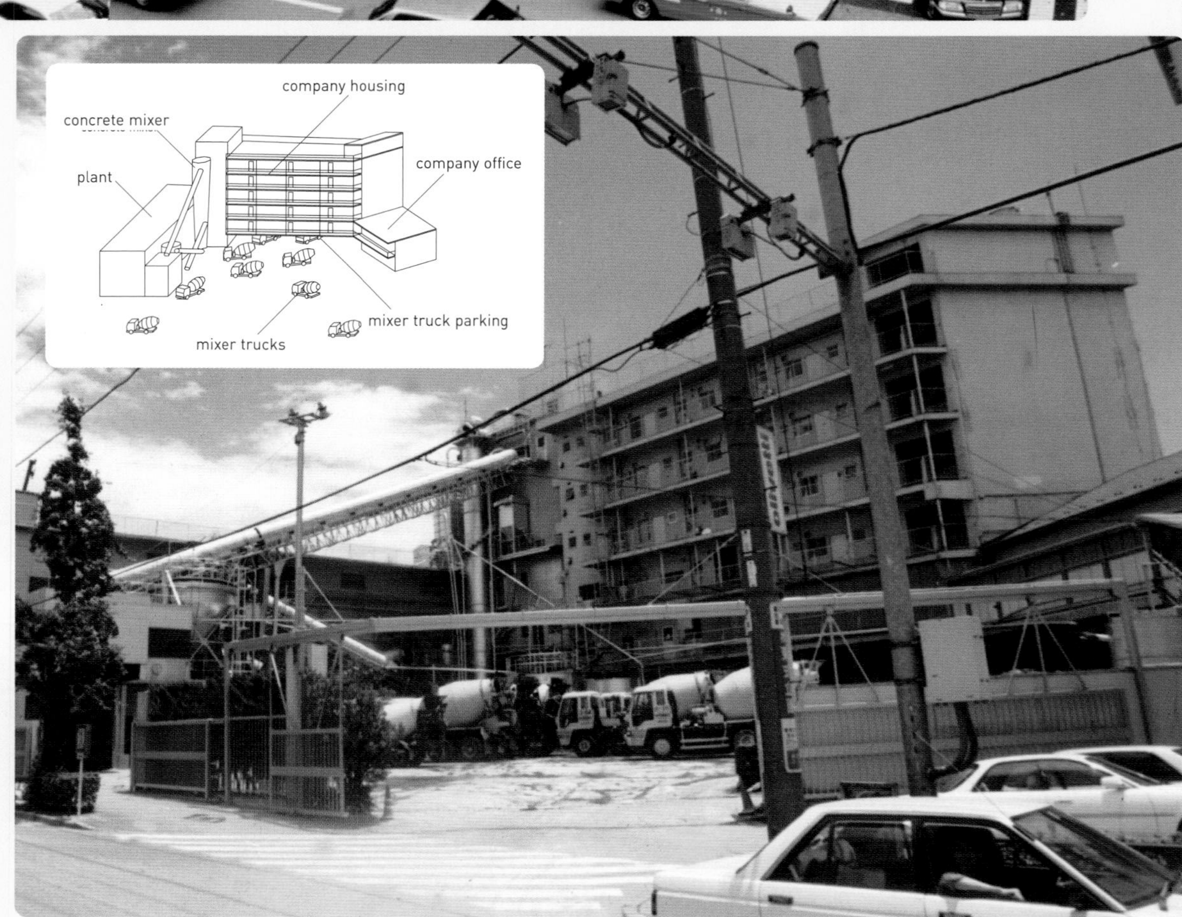

Above
Highway department store
Function: Expressway and department store
Site: Yurakucho, Chiyoda-ku and Ginza, Chuo-ku
The department store extends along a curving expressway, filling the site of what was previously the Shiodome river. Extending 500 metres, the store spreads over two floors. The expressway links to a row of lights from the underground parking facility. Incoming traffic from the car park obstructs the expressway with a tollgate.

Right
Nama-con apartment house
Function: Concrete batch plant and company housing
Site: Himon-ya, Meguro-ku
Aligned with Meguro Street, near the Daiei supermarket, the shiny silver concrete plant and the truck drivers' concrete housing are docked together. The mixers wait at the bottom of the plant to service the city. The packaging together of the work place and home creates a veritable man–machine system.

place; the buildings do not respond to cultural context and history. Their highly economically efficient answers are guided by minimum effort; in Tokyo such direct answers are expected. They are not imbued with the scent of culture; they are simply physical 'building'.

Moreover, Tokyo is a contradictory place, because it is these 'buildings' that in fact most clearly reflect the quality of urban space. The translation of issues of place through history and design seems like fabrication – this is Tokyo.

Where cultural interest is low, interest in practical issues is high. Whether civil engineering structures, roof tops, walls or gaps between buildings, whatever is at hand is utilised. What is important is the discovery of how to establish a second role for each environmental element, a doubling up that allows the reuse of spatial by-products. The material is not given, but is discovered through our own proposition of how to use it, something which might be termed 'affordance' of the urban environment. In addition, cross-categorical hybrids such as expressways and department stores can arise. Here, the department store depends on the expressway for its structure, and on the other hand the expressway depends on the department store for its validity in such a busy commercial area. Neither can exist on its own – they are interdependent.

Such existence seems anti-aesthetic, anti-historic, anti-planning, anti-classification. It releases the architecture of overdefinition towards generic 'building'. The buildings of Made in Tokyo are not necessarily after such ends but simply arrive at this position through their desperate response to the here and now. This is what is so refreshing about them.

Adjacency and 'Environmental Unit'

Our interest is in the diverse methods of making and using coherent environments within the city, together with the urban ecologies found there. This includes the unexpected adjacency of function created by cross-categorical hybrids, the coexistence of unrelated functions in a single structure, the joint utilisation of several differing and adjacent buildings and structures, or the packaging of an unusual urban ecology in a single building.

Within Tokyo's urban density are examples of a coherency that crosses over categorical or physical building boundaries. This is something that differs from the architecture of self-standing completeness. Rather, any particular building of this kind can perform several roles within multiple urban sets. These buildings cannot be specifically classified as architecture, or as civil engineering, city or landscape, thus we decided to call such coherent environments of adjacency 'environmental units'.

Cross-categorical hybrids such as expressways and department stores can arise. Here, the department store depends on the expressway for its structure, and on the other hand the expressway depends on the department store for its validity in such a busy commercial area. Neither can exist on its own – they are interdependent.

In Tokyo, the external envelope does not act to divide public and private, as in the traditionally understood idea of a facade. We are in a fluid situation, where rigid distinctions such as between shallowness and depth or front and back are easily overturned by a shift in the setting of the ecological unit.

The magnificent architecture of architects retains distinctions between categories, rationalises physical structure, pushes preconceived use on to that structure and tries to be self-contained, even though there are so many diverse ways in which to define environmental unities. It is a method that Modernism has passed down to us, and the precision of its ways is becoming stronger and stronger. Yet everyday life is made up of traversing various buildings. Living space is constituted by connections between various adjacent environmental conditions rather than by any single building. Can we draw out the potential of this situation and project this into the future? If so, it may be possible to counter the typical Japanese Modernist public facilities that are cut off from their surroundings and packaged into a single box. We can place attention on the issue of how usage (software) can set up a network, where public facilities can be dispersed into the city whilst interlapping with the adjacent environment. Spaces for living can penetrate into various urban situations and thereby set up new relations amongst them. The possibilities for urban dwelling expand.

Super car school
Function: Supermarket and driving school
Site: Kanamachi, Katsushika-ku
A driving school is planted on top of the double layer of the supermarket. The site includes parcels of other people's land that could not be purchased. This condition of the site, framed by the curve of the railway, is expressed directly in the extruded volume of the building. Above the entry ramp are framed the practice slopes for handbrake starts.

billboard
car
street lights
driving school car
practice slopes for handbrake starts
supermarket
金町自動車教習所
イトーヨーカドー

プロミス
Yen shop
武富士
パチスロタワー
777・777
パチスロ グリンピース
カラオケルーム
レイク
日焼けサロン
北の家族
アルファ

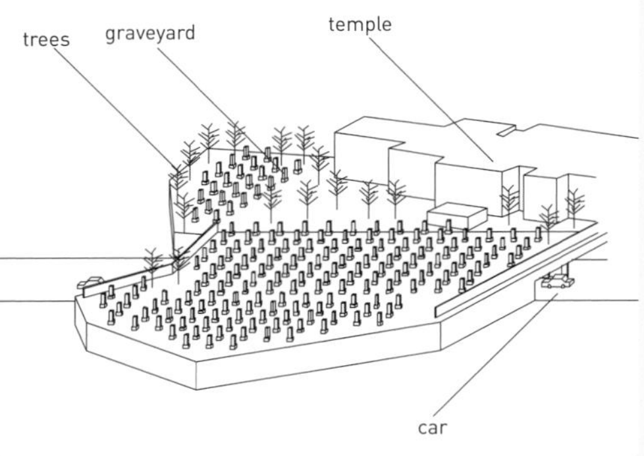
trees
graveyard
temple
car

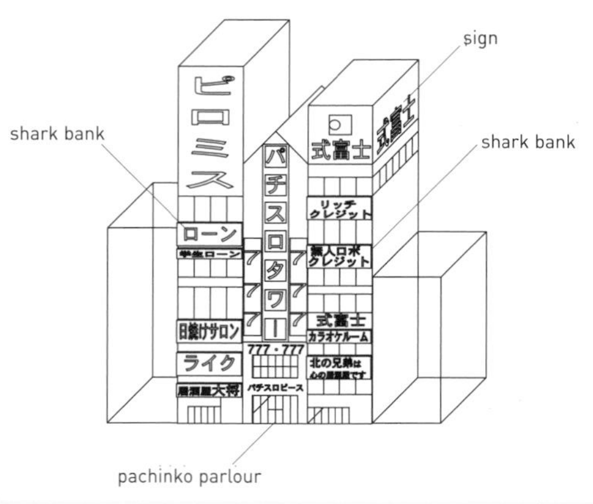
sign
shark bank
shark bank
pachinko parlour
ピロミス
パチスロタワー
式富士
ローン
日焼けサロン
ライク
777・777
カラオケルーム

On/Off

There is an overlapping of three orders that set up the 'environmental unit', based on category, structure and use. If we again take the example of the hybrid between expressway and department store, the traffic above and the shopping below simply share the same structure yet belong to different categories and have no use relation. In other words it is only structural order that unites the two. Maybe it is not that this example is impossible to evaluate within the existing cultural value system, but rather that the sense of unity is full of dubiousness – the essential reason why this example is da-me architecture.

We can say that when any of the three orders mentioned above are operating, they are 'on', whereas when they do not take effect they are 'off'. This system starts to incorporate all the value poles that seem to form such an important role in the recognition, and indeed the very existence, of da-me architecture. We can recognise that the examples of Made in Tokyo almost always comprise some aspect of being 'off'. In contrast to this, the magnificent buildings of architects are 'on', 'on', 'on'. Though the Parisian streetscape and the modern city are often held to be in opposition, the abundant examples of Made in Tokyo show that they are not necessarily bipolar. They simply exist within a score of 'on' and 'off'.

In any case, surely too much 'on' cannot be good for our mental landscape. If all three orders are switched 'on', there is only one possibility for achieving satisfying architecture. However, if we allow any or all aspects to be 'off', then suddenly the possibilities for variation explode to eight (two to the power of three). This establishes a huge release for designers. When we say that we can sense the pulse of Tokyo in the 'da-me architecture' that includes some aspect of being 'off', this means that even though the urban space of this city appears to be chaotic, in exchange, it contains a quality of freedom for production.

Furthermore, we hope in our design work to clearly represent possibilities for the urban future by being consistent with the principal findings of our research. Observations can only gain a certain clarity once they have been studied through design and vice versa. And such interactive feedback between observation and design is an efficient method through which to contribute to the city through the scale of architecture. AD

Translated by Marika Neustpny

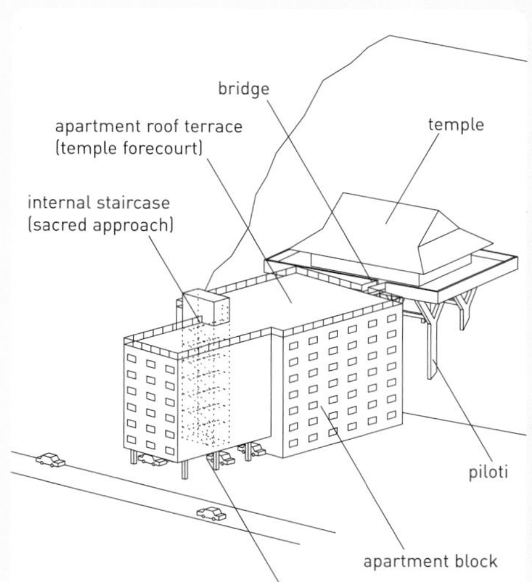

Opposite left
Pachinko Cathedral
Function: Pachinko Parlour and shark banks
Site: Kabuki-cho, Shinjuku
These are three separate buildings that take on the appearance of Paris's Notre Dame when viewed as a single entity. In the place of stone sculptures and reliefs, displaying scenes from the Bible, the complex pulses with information banners advertising its internal activities. The side tower buildings are almost completely let out to 'shark banks', loaning money at high interest rates. Here a biological system of the metropolis is formulated as a single symmetrical package – an endless cycle of losing money at the Pachinko Parlour, loaning money, only to lose it again.

Opposite right
Graveyard tunnel
Function: Graveyard and tunnel
Site: Sendagaya, Shibuya-ku
Around the area of the crossing of Killer Street and Stadium Street, the road slices under the temple graveyard. Nicknamed 'ghost tunnel', the Ikeda medium has named this a psychic spot.

Right
Apartment mountain temple
Function: Buddhist temple and private apartment housing
Site: Daimachi, Kanagawa-ku, Yokohama-shi
Near Tanmachi Station on the Toyoko train line is the Konpira Shrine. The ceremonial route passes the internal staircase of an apartment block, across the apartment roof and bridge to the main temple hall under waterproof sheeting.

Hyper Complex Living

Participating in the 'volatile aggregate' of the contemporary city, Japanese architect **Nobuyaki Furuya** has come to regard every building as an addition rather than an isolated object. With reference to his own projects, he explains how architecture might be performed as an acupuncture-like procedure, providing points in the urban chaos.

In his writings, Chuang-tzu, the Chinese mystic and philosopher of the 4th century BC, describes a king named Chaos. One day, Chaos invited the king of the south and the king of the north to a meal. As Chaos in fact did not have eyes or a nose, in return for the meal the two kings opened one orifice each day for Chaos, but he died the moment the seventh orifice was opened. The present-day Japanese word for 'chaos' (konton) has its roots in his name.

There are said to be three sources for research into chaos in the West: Poincare's problem of the motion of three or more astronomical bodies, Reynolds's problem of fluids, and the ergodic hypothesis of Boltzmann, all of which date from the second half to the end of the 19th century. In the 20th century, quantum theory and the theory of relativity took centre stage and chaos again began to attract attention only in 1963 when Lorenz published his work on heat convection currents. Interestingly, it was in that year that Arata Isozaki published *The Theory of Process Planning* on transformations in architecture.

We live in the extremely volatile aggregate called the contemporary city and attempt to deal with an extremely complex part of that aggregate called contemporary architecture.

We live in the extremely volatile aggregate called the contemporary city and attempt to deal with an extremely complex part of that aggregate called contemporary architecture. Modern architecture in the 20th century taught us to think of buildings as things standing in isolation in a characterless, transparent open space. However, an actual site has a surrounding environment, its own seasonal, social and cultural climates, and its own historical background. Any building, even one that is newly constructed, is in the nature of an addition, if we look at it in a broad context. Buildings are points in the chaos of the city. What I have in mind is using those points to perform on the city an acupuncture-like procedure.

Sendai Mediatheque Design Competition (1995)

This proposal is for a cultural complex containing a library, audiovisual library and exhibition space, designed with a total area of 20,000 square metres. The site faces Jozenjo-dori, a beautiful avenue lined with zelkova trees, in Sendai city. Except during the winter, the climate here is mild enough for people to stroll around without the need to separate the facility into three sections or layers according to individual functions. This would result in the building becoming a 'Forest of Media', encouraging visitors to enjoy encounters with unexpected persons or sources as they take a stroll inside.

All the books are controlled by computers, so visitors can read books and return them anywhere they like. These activities are expected to generate small features of various regions in one building, which like climate are always changing.

Railway Market in Bangkok (Research)

The 'railway market', a street in the suburbs of Bangkok, looks like a typical Asian market with its many stalls and bustling activity. However, suddenly a diesel-electric locomotive enters the scene. All stalls are shut up and the crowds dodge out of the way while it passes. As soon as the train has left, the situation is restored as before.

This solution is of a kind that we (=planer) never indicate. The reason for the sharing of this place as an exciting market and a railway is that it was never planned to be used in this way. It was not designed as a market. People find alternative ways with the passage of time.

Even great vortices (=chaos) can be traced back to small events. A small fracture can eventually lead to the destruction of an entire wall, and a slight error in copying genes can lead to the sudden emergence of a new species. When a new, unexpected activity comes into being, flourishes and establishes itself in a space that may not look like much at first glance, some event is likely to have provided the opportunity for this process to unfold.

The late John Hejduk was widely known to have valued 'beginnings' above all else. This was an expression of the fact that through continual abstraction he sought opportunities to 'poetically activate' the architectural spaces that Modernism had produced. The colonnade intended to eliminate the perception of a series of walls, the Mondrian-type plan suggestive of a square cut out of an infinitely extended space, free forms protruding from a wall – these were autonomous elements generated from the overall uniform space.

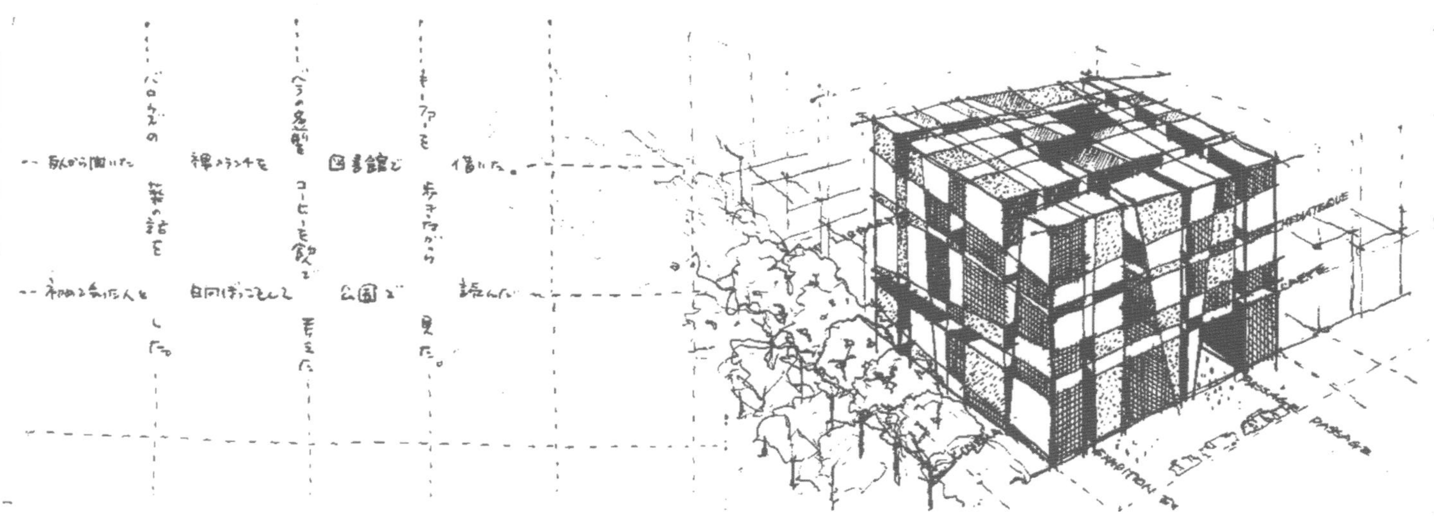

Mongolian Ger (Research)

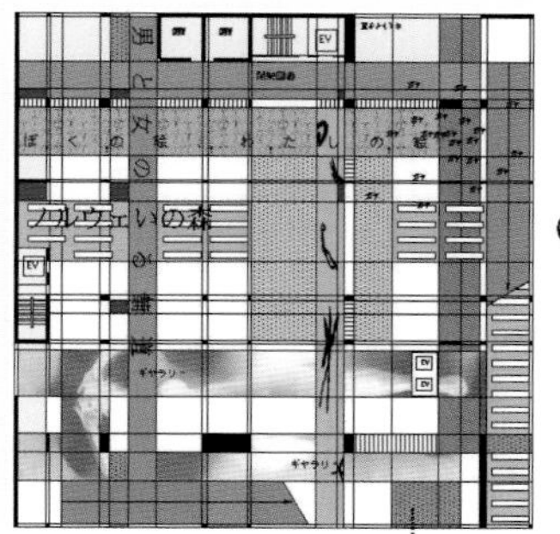

6F

The traveller rides his horse towards a yurt, which appears as a white dot in the grassland, like an oasis in the desert. This point of singularity, alone in a wide open space, draws people to it. It would be just a point of transition if other people were not there. If there is an encounter with other people, this may lead to new developments. Ultimately, architecture serves as a beginning, causing the unexpected encounter of people who were unrelated to one another until this point in time.

It can be said that the result is a city that has various problems stiffened, philosophically, by the concept of 'settling down'. It is necessary to distribute the house outside/inside the city, and the production function might have to be distributed in a similar manner. In addition, the media technology that develops rapidly might enable a decentralised residence that moves economically. This research investigates the possibility of a decentralised residence because it is assumed to be fluid, as is the city. The domestic animal is deployed to move household goods in a severe, natural environment: in the present age a Mongolian nomad looking at CNN and MTV can serve as a good case-study.

Hyper-Spiral Project (1996)

An Image of a highly three-dimensional city, Tokyo is proud of its efficiency and Asian chaotic accumulation yet, at the same time, is still beset by typical urban problems such as large quantities of waste, high energy consumption, a shortage of residential areas and traffic congestion. Also typical is the hindrance to settlement in its cultural centres due to the high costs of housing, while its traditional semidefined border conditions are slowly being eliminated by contemporary redevelopment projects.

In an attempt to make a city of international value, not only economically and politically but also in a cultural sense, places must remain for residents, culture and education. In this project, a 'highly three-dimensional' city is presented, made possible through the use of technology enabling construction to a height of 1,000 metres, and thereby enabling the amelioration of the city of Tokyo.

Conventionally, great investment is directed towards horizontal distribution and conveyance, at great expense both initially and through subsequent costs of maintenance of infrastructural systems like expressways throughout the city. The project attempts to decrease this horizontal transfer of commodities in favour of the vertical, and layers related services such as electricity generation and waste incineration or productive green space with consumer facilities for the distribution of products. This hyper-building is not a single towering high-rise building but a high-rise network with numerous ground-level entry points. It has no dead-ends of circulation or of infrastructure, and is easily accessible for restoration in the case of an emergency.

We call it the 'Hyper-Spiral' building based on its configuration of a double belt-like structure rising and intertwining in the form of a spiral.

Incremental Construction and Use

The chosen site surrounds Tokyo station, a culturally mature but sparsely populated area in the city centre. The three-dimensional city is to be constructed over the existing, without demolition, and constructed incrementally along with the conversion of the existing fabric to residential use.

Transportation systems of the Hyper-Spiral (local and semilocal rail lines, roads and pathways) are to be directly connected to the existing system: one end of the belt at the platform of Tokyo station, and the other leading to a point below ground to the metropolitan highway. In future, a new form of water-based transport, the Techno-Super Liner, will also easily be connected to this network.

The 13 pillars of the spiral's structural system have their foundations at the level of the metro station. Under present aerial restrictions, building heights are restricted to 300 metres but this is to be addressed in conjunction with the long-range development plan of an aerial traffic system. Initial construction of the Hyper-Spiral will be below this 300-metre restriction, and will later grow to its 1,000-metre height occupied by residences and other programmatic services utilising media technologies. It will be publicly owned and rented to private individuals and organisations, divided into smaller or larger units reserved in times of need for domestic, business or government, and also provide for common facilities such as schools and hospitals.

A Porous City

A transformation of the high-rise type built as a series of floor plates in a vertical box, inefficient in regards to ventilation and sunshine, will result in the Hyper-Spiral porous city. With many unoccupied spaces, semitransparent and allowing the passage of sun and air through the building, the Hyper-Spiral will create minimum shadow and allow the comfortable use of freed ground space. Within, the entire building forms a long, continuous easy slope, facilitating evacuation routes and waste disposal and recycling systems reaching from below ground to its highest points. Such a slope will also accommodate nonmotorised wheeled traffic such as bicycles and wheelchairs, and also the transfer of commodities and energy resources. The differential in air pressure over such a vertical distance may also be employed to this end.

Advantages of High-Rise Levels

More stable environmental conditions at the upper levels, such as continuous wind and lower fluctuations in temperature, are potential exploitable factors, as is the vertical layering of related activities of production, consumption and recycling. Thus garbage, prepared and composted, fertilises upper horticultural spaces, and this more compact model of a contained cycle is to be similarly employed in the use of air and water collected from the surrounding sky. Conveyance is to be reduced to a minimum in favour of local purification, use and recycling. Towards this end, the structure of the building itself, the 'sponge core', has the ability to retain water, provide a pipeless infrastructure and decrease vibration. It is a second ground soil and employs mechanisms for recycling resources, power generation and resource purification.

Hyper-Pillars

The V-shaped pillars, called 'hyper-pillars', form not only the structural system but also that of necessary systems of vertical conveyance and emergency services. Each standing point of the pillar is below the centre of gravity of its load, with the conveyance systems arranged around it to rapidly carry people or commodities between the ground and the upper levels.

The Fins and the Sky-Canyon

The fins of the slabs are settled at a pitch of 7.5 metres around the whole of the sponge core. Between them, numerous subdivisions are possible, creating two-storey units in a domino system in the air, and providing smaller-scale areas for residential use or any other activity requiring sunshine and views. In contrast to this is the large void space between the cores, the 'Sky-Canyon', which may be used for larger-scale interior units.

Circulation

Transport within the Hyper-Spiral is of various ranges and speeds, employing multideck elevators leading to the ground, sky trams within the building, conveyors, skywalks and corridors. The multideck elevator linking the upper storeys with the ground is a particularly large and rapid conveyance system, which can exist at any pillar and reach any floor. It is a 60-metre chain of 7 to 8 units, 7.5 metres long (the height of the fin) that reaches ground level and the existing metro system, which are connected horizontally by the sky-tram systems. This is the main traffic system within the building and is hung from the base of the sponge core at 5,000-metre intervals. It can then be connected to the existing transportation system in the long-range plan.

The City of the Next Generation

We are now aware of the meaninglessness and futility of building high-rise buildings for the competitive sake of their height alone, and it is not the purpose of the project to simply achieve a 1,000 metres benchmark. What is the goal, however, is a city that is three-dimensional and porous. This image of the city will demonstrate how we may arrest the incessantly spreading city, while creating a new stage for urban culture in the next generation. ◿D

We are now aware of the meaninglessness and futility of building high-rise buildings for the competitive sake of their height alone, and it is not the purpose of the project to simply achieve a 1,000 metres benchmark. What is the goal, however, is a city that is three-dimensional and porous. This image of the city will demonstrate how we may arrest the incessantly spreading city, while creating a new stage for urban culture in the next generation.

Gaikoku Mura:
Japanese Foreign Country Villages

ANA
ANA

Photographing the Gaikoku Mura foreign country villages in Japan is part of an ongoing project for photographer **Sue Barr**. Her photographs challenge the popular stereotypical view of the villages as architecturally insignificant leisure parks, as well as the wider Western perception of the Japanese as purveyors of cultural reproduction, whether in fashion, music or design. Bringing images such as those of a replica of Stratford-on-Avon at Maruyama Shakespeare Park back to London for an exhibition at the Architectural Association, she was able to question the viewers' understanding of what constitutes a fake.

Previous spread
Huis Ten Bosh Dutch Village, Nagasaki, Japan.

Opposite
Marksburg Castle, Ueno German Culture Village, Okinawa, Japan.

Above
Aerial view of herb garden, Maruyama Shakespeare Park, Chiba, Japan.

During the economic bubble of the late 1980s, Gaikoku Mura foreign country villages began to appear throughout Japan. These were developed as a means of revitalising regional economies and feeding Japan's interest in foreign cultures.

Gaikoku Mura – Japanese for foreign country village – is a specific type of cultural park found only in Japan. Examples range from Canada World and Swiss Village in Hokkaido to Russian Village in Niigata and Huis Ten Bosch in Kyushu, which is an ecologically sound modern city albeit one disguised as a 17th-century Dutch village.

These parks, which are all too often dismissed as theme parks, particularly from a European perspective where the term is associated with roller coasters and childish amusement rides, actually display a high degree of sophistication in their reproductions, though they are replicas of a Europe that exists only as an image. All exhibit a detailed rendering of the vernacular architecture of the country in question, and extend this re-creation to include national people, produce, musicians and performers, all of which work together to enhance the educational value of the parks.

Glucks Königreich in Hokkaido used 400-year-old paving stones imported from Berlin and Dresden, and includes a full-scale reproduction of the Buckenburg Castle in Bavaria. The Maruyama Shakespeare Park in Chiba is a re-creation of the house in Stratford-on-Avon where Shakespeare was born, and is an exact replica of how the house would have looked in Shakespeare's time; traditional building materials, methods and skilled craftspeople have been employed in its construction. Due to the high attention to detail, its designers claim that it is as authentic as the original house, standing thousands of miles away in Stratford, which has suffered 300 years of deterioration. The house in Chiba is 'unsullied by the passage of time and the changes of the later occupants'.

It has been argued that Gaikoku Mura evolved to enable Japanese tourists to experience authentic glimpses of a foreign culture without the hassles of leaving Japan, but this stereotype simply further perpetuates misunderstandings of the complexity of Japanese culture.

The extraordinary levels of attention to detail elevate Gaikoku Mura to a new form of cultural reproduction and challenge our preconceived ideas of authenticity. Repackaging culture as a leisure activity has blurred the lines between education and entertainment. ▫

In the age of Indeterminacy — Towards a Non-visual Pragmaticism

Hong Kong architect **Gary Chang** advocates a framework for a pragmatic reading of the intensified city. Four of Chang's projects are illustrated below, putting theory into practice and elaborating on such themes as immaterialism, connection, change and coexistence.

Conditions: How the City Intensifies

Intensity describes the state of things, literally a kind of immaterial density that pervades the city as a general culture. It is vigorous yet does not necessarily embody a physical form. On the one hand, the extreme form of urban intensity is represented by the massiveness and rapid occurrence of (and between) individual events. This particularly refers to events of gigantic scale that disappear without trace.

Below we propose a framework of reading based on four concepts – change, choice, connection and coexistence – to further elaborate the idea of intensified city with reference to Hong Kong. These are not in sequence, nor do they represent any hierarchy. They are in relationship with one another, though the relationship is not explicitly linear.

Each of the four concepts is not strictly a cause nor an effect of the phenomena identified below, but they do provide some relevant points of reference to understand the local phenomena.

Change

Force is the immaterial cause of change. Cityscape is a product of an infinite number of different forces coming into play at the same point in time. Social, economic, political, cultural or historical forces act from different directions, and the change that results is directional, pointing to ideals about the urban space. After all, change is about the survival of society.

In addition, the concept of change is intricately associated with time. Time is a distinctive dimension that has its own internal logic of space: a space that is not measured in a physical sense but by an immaterial calibration – duration. As physical space provides a medium of locating objects, time provides a medium for changes to take place. Yet unlike an object that occupies space, there is no full saturation of time. The intensity of change can be infinite, always offering the possibility for further intensification with various scales and durations.

Forces are generated from shifting concerns and ideals in the course of time. They are external factors yet can cause implosions within a system. Though it is possible to identify the sources of the forces, it is always oversimplifying to reduce the cause of change to one single force. Change has no final form, only intermediate products in the process of transformation. Change does not necessarily lead to growth or unidirectional progresses, however the shifting of forces and the subsequent transformation of systems present.

Connection

Connection is about constructing relationships between systems. System varies in scale and nature, and presents along the spectrum between polarities, be this physical or virtual, micro or macro. A beeping sound in the underground train during rush hour can induce a phone search by the crowd. The system of wireless communication acts on the system of public space. Altogether such a scenario reflects the issue of congestion, mass displacement, collective behaviour and pattern of living. Here, connection is an instrument that relates a matrix of references.

Connection confirms the presence of a boundary by which relationships are created between two or more disparate entities. Or in other words, boundary separates and at the same time connects. The fluidic nature of boundary shifts, dissolves and associates with distant elements or phenomena, creating an intensive spatial montage.

Connection is created through the implemented interface. It creates a platform for interaction. The peripheral plane is itself the connecting device, triggering unforeseen spatial experience and a subversive visual–information relationship that animates the presumably static public space.

Connection evokes a network of conjunction. Space flows in a fluidic manner and is not constrained by an independent edifice. It results in a separate system while hybridising with other existing systems.

Connection in its most brutal manner is revealed in the act of overlapping and penetration. Surfaces multiply by the making of additional layers and entities. Every surface is maximised to enhance visual connection and, eventually, to raise its commercial value through the amount of visual contact.

Choice

Choice is a representation of both individual and collective desire. Selection is a responsive act allowing for the identification of existing potentials and giving room for the reconfiguration of possible outcomes. This is something that often leads to a transgression of the norms through deviations from the usual path.

Choice can be regulated but cannot be completely controlled. It is provided through a matrix of consideration in which the existing conditions as well as the imposed forces are taken into account.

Choice unveils the power of creativity of the public to achieve what is often misunderstood as given. Looking at the process of selection, individual vision can be reorganised and reformulated from the fragments. While the external and internal constraints are revealed through the reading of individual choices, a maximum of possibilities can also be attained through creating flexibility under the same conditions.

Coexistence

Coexistence enhances a mix to become a total system. A rough view of Hong Kong is like a single whole with hiatuses carved out from the monolithic city-building mass. Zooming in, it is composed of fragments of events and physicalities. We call these urban fragments (city bytes}. Often, they are in huge quantities and scales, with a great variety of life spans. They are self-developing at all times. The richness of these city bytes is generated through collective creativity. They invade every part of the city, transforming the original use of space and revitalising the dead areas of the city. Sometimes they are totally planned.

The coexisting approach favours adaptation instead of imposition, reuse instead of erasure, diversity instead of homogeneity. Thus city bytes are highly adaptive because they are generated from specific urban conditions. They respect the existing conditions and seek the neglected potential of those conditions. They fragmentise the overstructured city and provide new energy to fuel its self-generation. Coexistence is a viable strategy for the development from ambition to economy.

Coexistence is an open system that operates as a means to urban sustainability. In contrast to evolution, which is a transformation within one entity, sustainability transforms with a network of interrelated systems that work as a totality of difference.

Conclusion

The above discussion is an attempt to delineate the logic of a city's operation where efficiency and intensity result through a more improvised than structured model. Though the three-dimensional cityscape is breathtaking, it is the non-visual-based pragmatism behind that effects such realisation. After all, it is this 4-C approach that is able to avoid any kind of preclusive visualisation of an urban landscape, and more importantly allows for an ultimate escape from any disguised ambition of an ideal city.

living / working / eating / sleeping / chatti
eating / sleeping / chatting / dressing / re
chatting / dressing / reading / living / wor
reading / living / working / eating / sleepin
working / eating / sleeping / chatting / dre

Gary Chang, My Own Apartment, Hong Kong, China, 1998

The bachelor dwells within a squeezed space of 330 square feet. A compact and efficient arrangement of kitchenette, bathroom and laundry area liberates the remaining space for the various programmes of bachelor life. The dominance of white, translucent and transparent materials, in combination with changing ambient lighting, all seemingly begin to 'dematerialise' the apartment.

In contrast, the only full-height object is the tower of solid cherry-wood that incorporates the movie projector, refrigerator and kitchen, wash basins and laundry machines. Ultimate spatial flexibility is created through the multiple operations of the partitions, lighting and mobile furniture. All the mundane necessities of bachelor life – books, CDs, clothing, pictures, stereo, videos – are stacked on a chrome factory-shelving system and hidden discreetly behind floating white curtains. The central space becomes the actual space for living/working/eating/sleeping/chatting/dressing/reading. Blue fluorescent tubes are carefully placed to wash the floor with an unearthly glow, while bright uplighting articulates structural members.

The main aperture of the front window offers different 'views' to the world beyond – the actual view out of the window or 'through' the large-scale movie screen to the fantasy world of Hollywood, the real world of news or the electronic world of the Internet.

Imagine. During the day a couple stays in the Suitcase. They could open up all the sliding partitions and enjoy a totally indoor open space with a dimension of 44 metres x 5 metres. Later in the day they might listen to music in the music chamber, read a book in the library or meditate on the glazed floor. In the evening the entire space turns into a lounge for parties, celebrations and other events. Rooms can then be gradually formulated when night falls.

Suitcase House Hotel, Badaling Shuiguan, Beijing, 2001–2002

Suitcase House Hotel originated from the experimental development the Commune by the Great Wall in Beijing. The developers of the project invited 12 younger-generation Asian architects, from South Korea, Japan, Taiwan, Singapore, Thailand, mainland China and Hong Kong, to independently design 11 houses and a club in the valley at the foot of the Great Wall. The development consists of two phases. The first phase of the Commune is a guesthouse-hotel community while the second phase will be weekend villa-homes.

Casting a question mark on the proverbial image of the house, Suitcase House Hotel attempts to rethink the nature of intimacy, privacy, spontaneity and flexibility. It is a simple demonstration of the desire for ultimate adaptability, in pursuit of a proscenium for infinite scenarios, a plane of sensual (p)leisure.

The dwelling represents a stacking of strata. The middle stratum embodies a reincarnated *piano nobile par excellence* for habitation, activity and flow. Adapting a nonhierarchical layout with the help of mobile elements provided by the envelope, it transforms itself readily according to the nature of the activities, number of inhabitants and personal preferences for degrees of enclosure and privacy. A metamorphic volume, it slides effortlessly from an open space to a sequence of rooms, depending on the inhabitants' specific requirements. Each room is then differentiated by the provision of a unique amenity.

The bottom stratum acts as a container for dedicated spaces. Compartments are concealed by a landscape of pneumatically assisted floor panels. At any point in time only the essential elements required will have a spatial presence. Apart from the basic chambers of bedroom, bathroom, kitchen and storage, there are a series of chambers for specific use and mode: a meditation chamber (with a glazed floor looking down the valley below), music chamber, library, study and lounge, as well as a fully equipped sauna.

Imagine. During the day a couple stays in the Suitcase. They could open up all the sliding partitions to enjoy a totally indoor open space with a dimension of 44 metres x 5 metres. Later in the day they might open up a series of chambers according to their mood, for example to listen to music in the music chamber, read a book in the library or meditate on the glazed floor. In the evening, when more guests arrive, the entire space turns into a lounge for parties, celebrations and other events. Rooms can then be gradually formulated when night falls. A maximum of seven guest rooms could be formed, which could accommodate up to 14 guests if the party goes on till late and they need to stay overnight.

The envelope is a stratification of vertical layers. The outer skin is a wrap of full-height double-glazed folding doors while the inner layer comprises a series of screens forming a matrix of openings. The abstract facade pattern is thereby rooted in its user-oriented operational logic. The dwelling is provided with multiple entrances, each with equal status, and each leading to a rereading of the spatial organisation.

To blur the boundaries between house, interior and furniture, the entire structure and elements are monotonically clad in timber inside and outside of the steel structure supported by, and cantilevered out from, the concrete base. They also house facilities including a pantry, maid's quarter, boiler room and the sauna.

The dwelling is located at the head of the Nangou Valley. To maximise views to the prominent Great Wall and solar exposure in the continental temperate climate, a north–south orientation has been adopted. It is possible to see the Great Wall from all major spaces within the dwelling, and also from the totally free and unobstructed roof terrace that is accessed from below via a pull-down staircase.

Mega iAdvantage Datacentre,
Chai Wan, Hong Kong, 1999–2001

Mega iAdvantage, the first dedicated high-rise datacentre in Asia, is located in an old industrial area in Hong Kong Island East. Constructed on foundations originally intended for another building, the 33-storey datacentre was completed in just 380 days after design inception. In terms of spatial allocation it has a hardware to person ratio of 7:3. The development of the project was 'organic' in so far as the programme evolved during the course of construction.

In terms of the design approach, the datacentre demonstrates our interest in fundamental architectural elements. Surface is the primary element that visually defines the material presence. The formation of surface and its subsequent breakdown into zones, loops and lines are also explored.

Given the limited time available and the absence of a frozen brief, we consider the datacentre not as a single project but as a summation of all the possible projects generated on this plot of land. Under this 'mutating' brief, Mega iAdvantage is categorised into 'the Facade Project – surface experiment'; 'the Lobby Project – zone experiment'; 'the Typical Floor Project – loop experiment'; and 'the Headquarters Project – line experiment'. The series of experiments are an attempt to rethink the relationship between spatiality and materiality through the extensive use of reflectivity, transparency and opacity.

The Facade Project

To ease the construction process within the time constraint, indentation of the building mass is minimised, resulting in a rectangular block with a podium following the site boundary. The building envelope is divided into five surfaces: four facades and a podium. Each is designed with its own autonomous logic and results in a diversity of visual impressions depending on the direction of approach. The main (south) facade is clad in industrial corrugated-steel panels with standardised aluminium ribbon windows, which gives a shiny effect in the afternoon sun. A graphic pattern of vertical strips in inexpensive ceramic tile is applied on the east facade. The west facade, which is visible only from afar, is finished in texture spray paint with a huge signboard on the roof. The least prominent rear facade is designed in black tile. The streamline podium is covered with black perforated aluminium panels with silver supergraphics and a translucent Plexiglass light-wall at street level.

The Lobby Project

The main lobby comprises linear zones that suggest a perpendicular direction of movement. Two gigantic free-form objects, one in timber, the other in aluminium, are designed as security zones. The former acts as a security partition with a waiting bench while the latter incorporates surveillance equipment. The other linear zones are the gallery, entrance, lift lobby and the building-management control centre. The drastically different touches for each zone provide a montage of various spatialities in the small lobby space.

The Headquarters Project

The headquarters, Megatop, located on the top two floors, is conceived as an interplay of fins (a wire-frame model) and surfaces with a variety of transparencies. These spaces are generated from a matrix of lines. All surfaces become abstract from afar, while their materiality emerges at close proximity.

Starting from the double-space atrium, the lines form the outer layer of the internal facade and run three-dimensionally along the longitudinal axis. The line pattern varies in different areas and in different materials including aluminium fins, steel baffles, carpets, silkscreen glass and acoustic panels. Within this simulated 'wire frame' stands a glass box housing the network operation centre of the corporation. The hardware zones are located on the lower level while the office spaces are stacked on top with an internal ramp connecting the two.

The Typical Floor Project

Floors containing hardware find expression in a rhythm of alternate loops of reflective materials (mirrors and galvanised-steel sheets) and timber. Variations in reflectivity animate the movement along the 50-metre-long corridor.

M&E Design

Mega iAdvantage involves very sophisticated electrical and mechanical facilities. In order to solve the problems of electromagnetic disturbance, the plant rooms are centrally located on the ground floor, podium and roof. Back-up generators and uninterruptible power supply (UPS) are equipped to ensure normal operation in case of power failure. The FM200 and Inergen gaseous flooding firefighting systems have been carefully arranged according to the distribution of electrical and mechanical facilities. Air-conditioning design is also a prior consideration. The indoor temperature and relative humidity must be constantly maintained at 2–20°C and 10–50 per cent respectively.

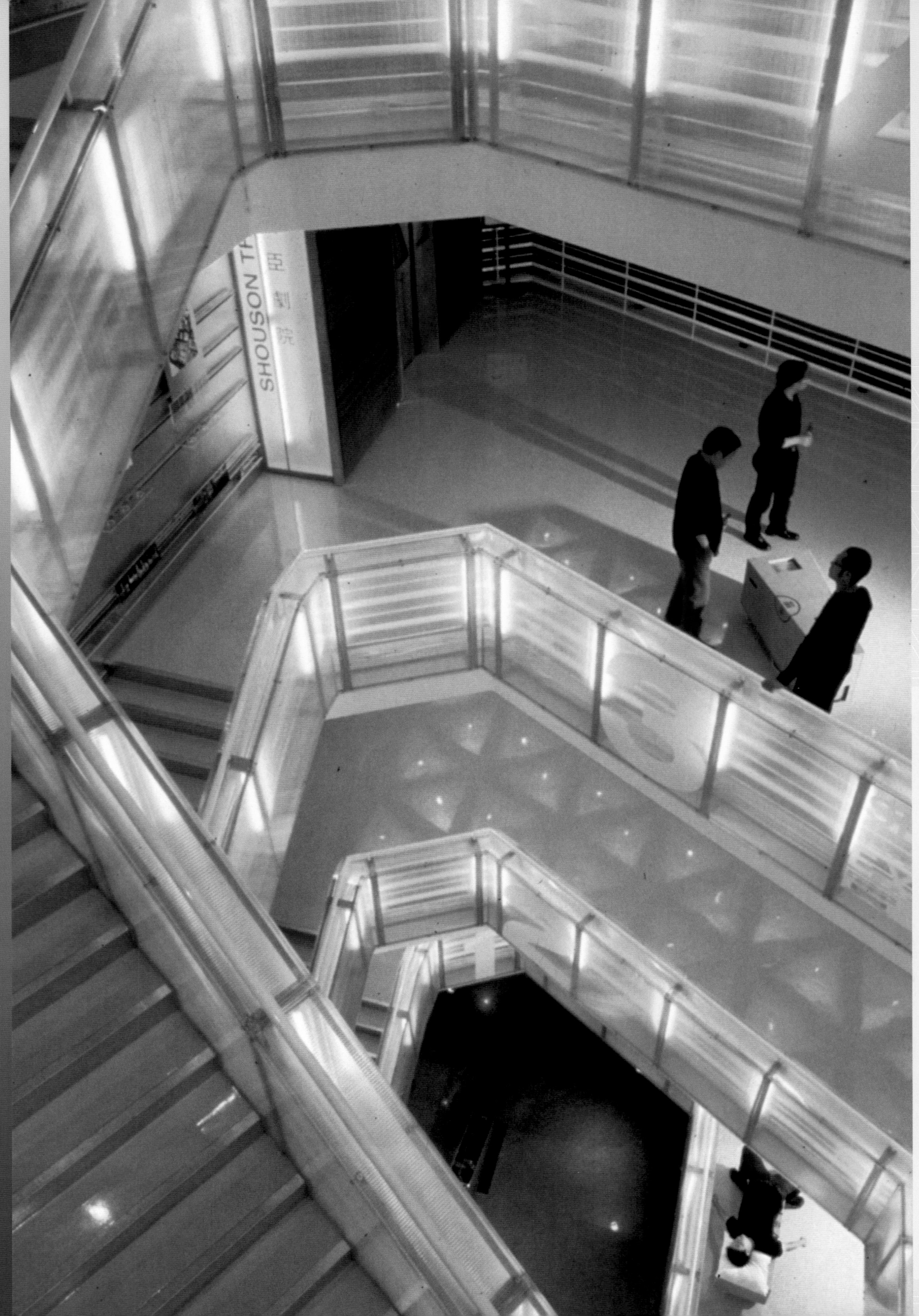
SHOUSON
臣劇院

Hong Kong Arts Centre Renovation, 1999–2000

Within the constrained conditions of an existing structure, and under an extremely tight budget, this project attempts to redefine the space of the approximately 700 square metres of floor area of the atrium of the Hong Kong Arts Centre. Four storeys high, the atrium, which is composed of various foyers to different performance spaces, is underused for most of the time. Our idea is to open up the opportunities for this formerly leftover space by inserting different flexible programmes and to achieve a crossover between bar (leisure), retail facilities (shopping) and exhibition (art) without disturbing the integrity of the multilevel space.

The first layer of the renovation is to transform the whole internal wall into a continuous skin covered with metallic paint. A pattern of horizontal metal channels is attached on top of the wall to connect the different parts of the foyer, as well as providing a system to display art work and to install different accessories such as table-top brochure holders. To further enhance full flexibility, a series of mobile units are placed throughout different floors to inhabit the space according to different functional requirements.

Finally, a light box is built on top of the existing stair balustrade, forming a continuous spiral of white light that connects the whole project. The light-box balustrade, embracing the existing handrails, also becomes a gigantic spiral directory for easy orientation to the performance spaces. The entrances become floating planes made of horizontal aluminium louvres with a plane of yellow light separating them from the wall. Another layer of suspended wires supports light fixtures highlighting the existing waffle structure. A layer of high-level movable cantilever target lights on the wall channels forms another datum specially dedicated to the illumination of art works during exhibitions. The glossy epoxy floor at all levels gives a neutral touch to the atrium in general while making the information sandwiched between the channel wall and the light box stand out. Along the passage from ground floor to fourth floor, the renovated atrium becomes a site in which intensified events can take place. ᗡ

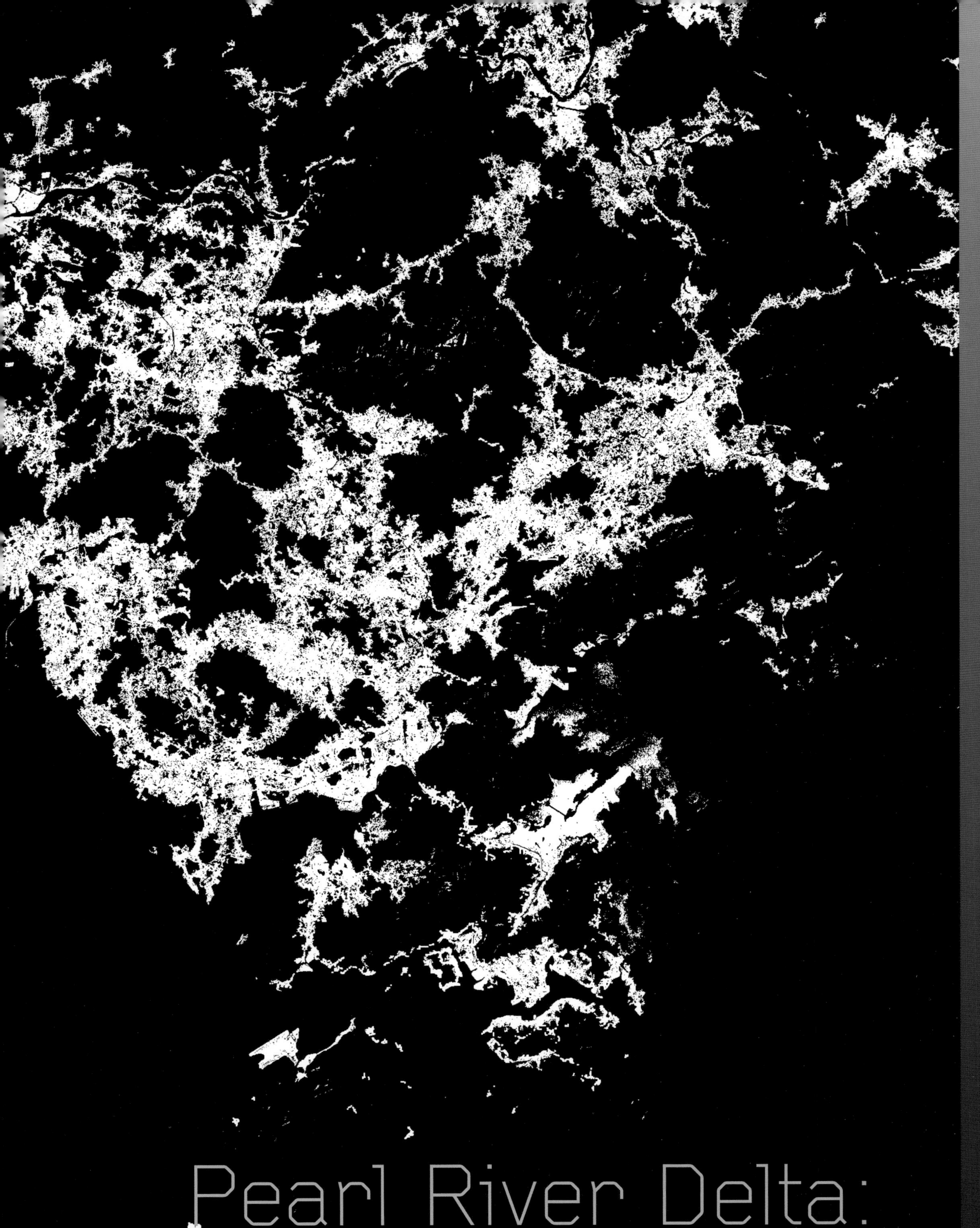

Pearl River Delta:
Lean Planning, Thin Patterns

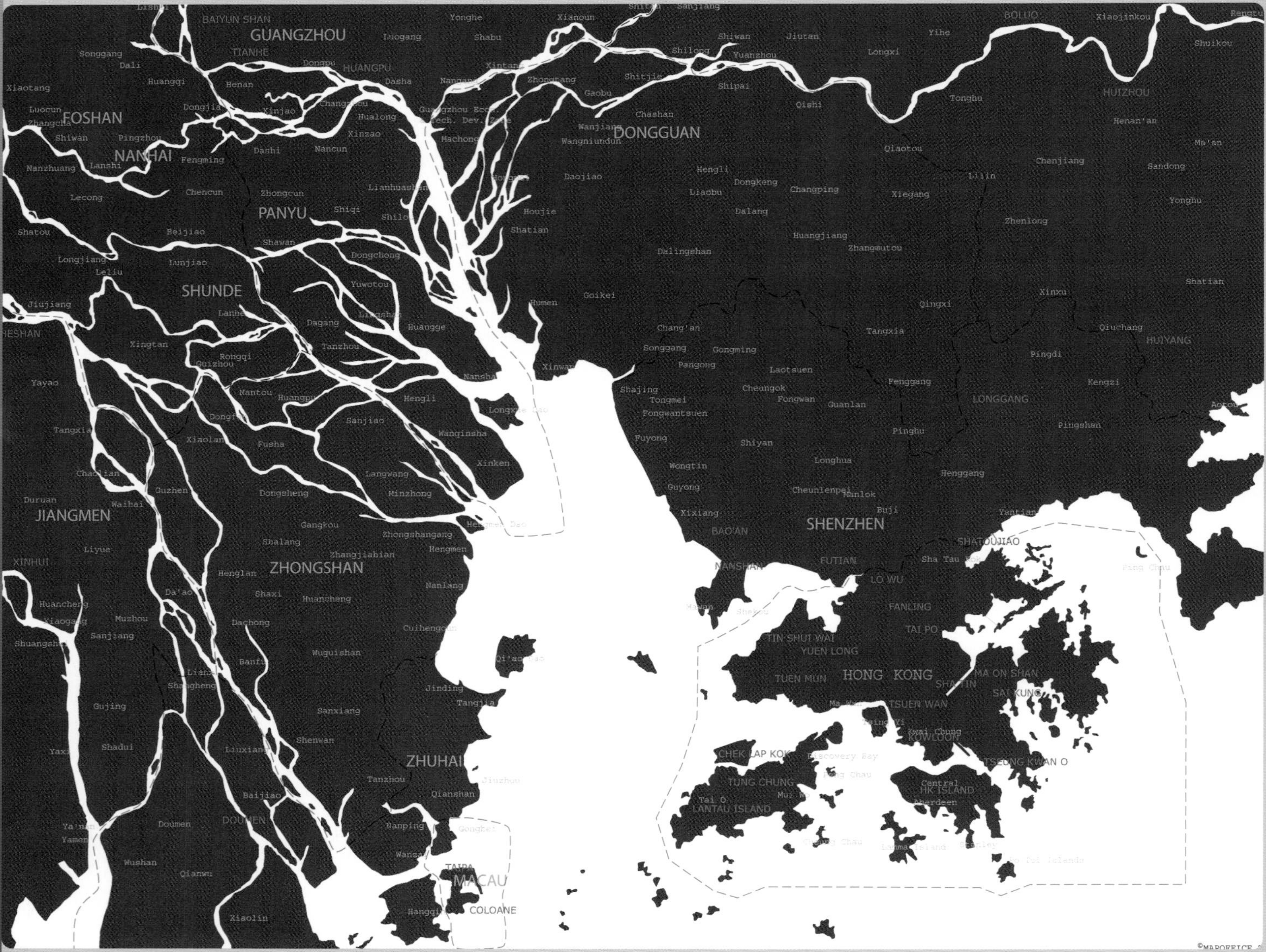

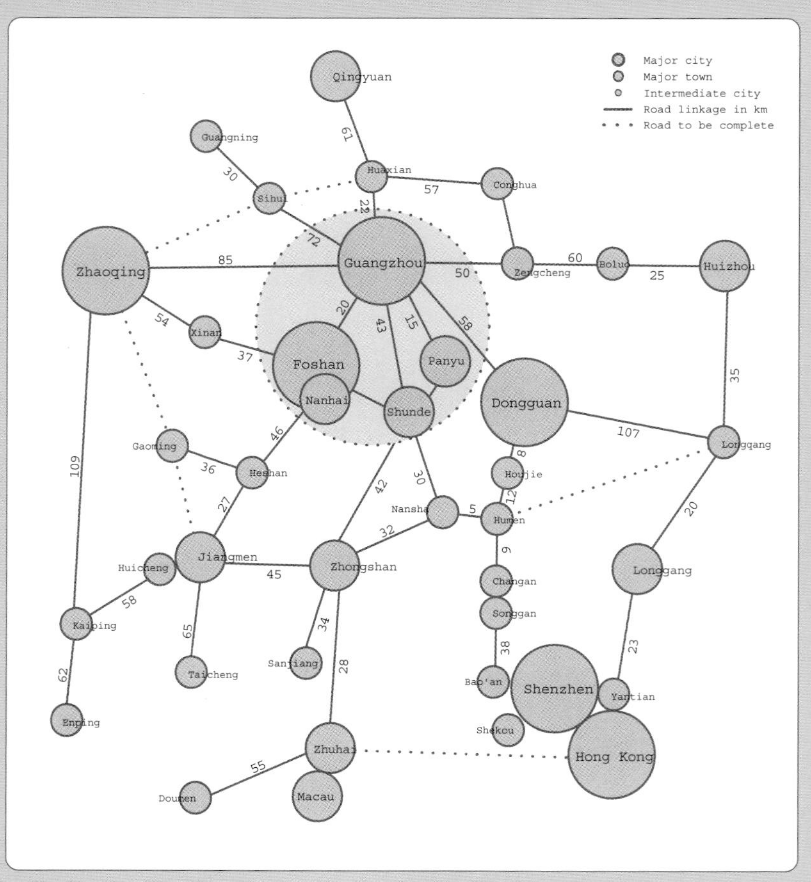
Major city
Major town
Intermediate city
Road linkage in km
Road to be complete
Qingyuan
Guangning
Huaxian
Conghua
Sihui
Zhaoqing
Guangzhou
Zengcheng
Boluo
Huizhou
Xinan
Foshan
Nanhai
Panyu
Shunde
Dongguan
Gaoming
Heshan
Longqang
Houjie
Nansha
Humen
Huicheng
Jiangmen
Zhongshan
Changan
Longgang
Kaiping
Songgan
Taicheng
Sanjiang
Bao'an
Shenzhen
Yantian
Enping
Shekou
Zhuhai
Hong Kong
Doumen
Macau
61
30
57
22
72
85
60
50
25
54
20
43
15
58
37
35
46
107
36
8
30
12
109
27
42
5
32
9
45
20
58
34
65
38
28
23
62
55

Based in Hong Kong, French architects **Laurent Gutierrez** and **Valérie Portefaix** of MAP Office run a collaborative studio that incorporates architecture and the visual arts. Here, they describe their current research into 'lean planning', which focuses on the impact of economic production and distribution specifically in the 'Made in China' or Pearl River Delta region of southern China.

> The southern China metropolis, only vaguely perceived in most of the world at this time, is likely to become the most representative urban face of the twenty-first century.
> — Manuel Castells[1]

The purpose of this essay is to characterise a region harshly described by Rem Koolhaas as 'an urban condition free of urbanity'.[2] In reality, the expression of this new form of urbanity and spatial condition related to the notion of development is embedded in specific cycles of production and distribution. As a consequence, the dynamic and multidimensional forces that spread across the surface of the territory are to be explored and qualified. Those characteristics, visible traces marking the land, appear as paradigms of contemporary civilisation, and are evident in the simple inventory of a commodified society labelled 'Made in China'.

The new capitalist mode of production succumbs to the process of globalisation, not only from an economic and political viewpoint, but also through empirical knowledge. Therefore, the genealogy of the Pearl River Delta (PRD) appears as progressive creative forces of development. In this particular context, the multiple processes of constructing a system that includes an infinite addition of layers encounter fields of reflection that are theoretically and ideologically expressed by Postmodernism as the fate of an epoch. Corresponding to the characteristics of this moment, and because of its particular history and geography, the PRD represents a synthesis of universal elements belonging to a global flow but with the specifics of a local territory.

1 Delta Geography

Asset 1 – Delta Land

Formed by the convergence of three rivers, the PRD is a transitional space between land and sea, where water – through the silt and debris it carries – has extended the land into the sea. This form of growth by gradual external addition, fusion or inclusion indicates that accreted material can be either distinct or melt as part of an increasing homogeneous body. Accretion – the three-dimensional adding, piling and layering of unrelated material – has many implications when it comes to interpreting the structure of the land and the potential to plan it. Environment and landscape are transformed under a multitude of pressures – natural, artificial and immaterial – and these transformations affect not only the stability of the ground but anything planned onto/into it.

Accretion shapes and monitors human activities. In this condition, regulation of flow, control of water levels to protect land that has been gained from the sea, irrigation and drainage, control of sand and salt components, are the first preconditions for introducing life and developing the liquid land into a network of settlements. This series of actions on the one hand presents an open system capable of generating new land, but has also contributed to a high degree of instability and uncertainty in the region.

Study 1 – Port

The regional marine transport network is intrinsically related to social and economic growth. In 1757, port cities were the sole places where trading with the West was accepted, turning Guangzhou and smaller cities into hectic trade centres. Due to both domestic and foreign trade, these cities rapidly developed into a powerful international commercial network. At present, more than 40 million containers pass through the PRD every year, making the region the world's busiest/largest port.

As the physical centre of the region, the Pearl River is a place characterised by intense and dynamic activities. Busy to the extreme, water provides the infrastructure for various marine traffic, such as ferries, liners, crane barges (lighters) and container cargo. Divided into parking, roads and highways to segregate different kinds of vessels, the harbour is a medium for transporting both men and merchandise.

Outline 1 – Accretion

How to read what is not yet written? How can we understand a condition that is lived by millions of people, but still not completely materialised? Space is inundated. It is not possible to distinguish exactly what is land and what is floating, what is built and what is vegetation, what is building material and what is

Previous spread
Population densities in the Pearl River Delta region.

Opposite and next page
Delta population
Guangdong's population is bound to the same regional strength, a place traditionally open to foreign exchange and non-Chinese trade. The majority of the overseas Chinese population originates from this region and has progressively built a powerful and strategic network to expand this system abroad.

Top
Pearl River Delta region.

Bottom
Urban network in the Pearl River Delta region.

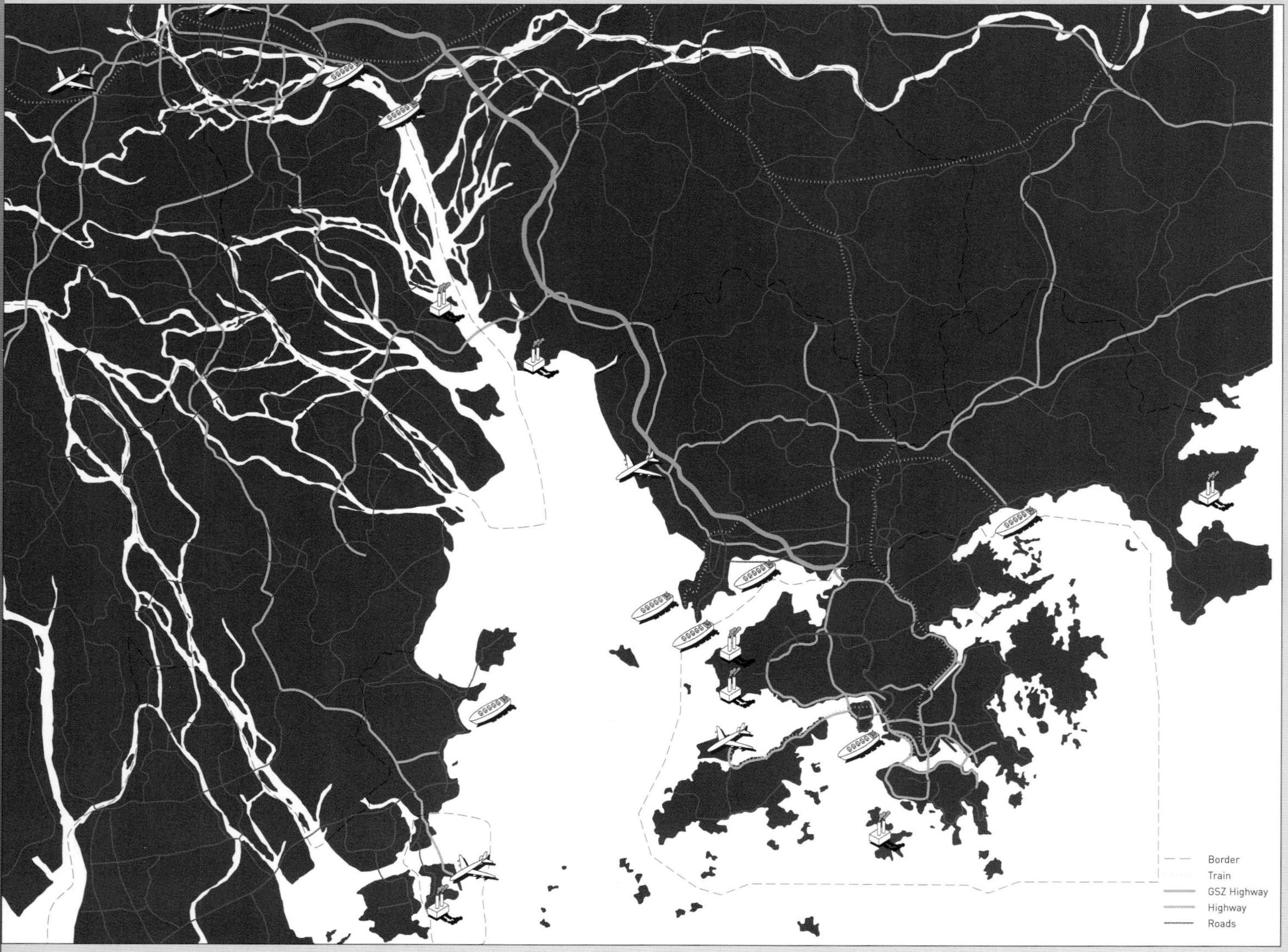

Border
Train
GSZ Highway
Highway
Roads

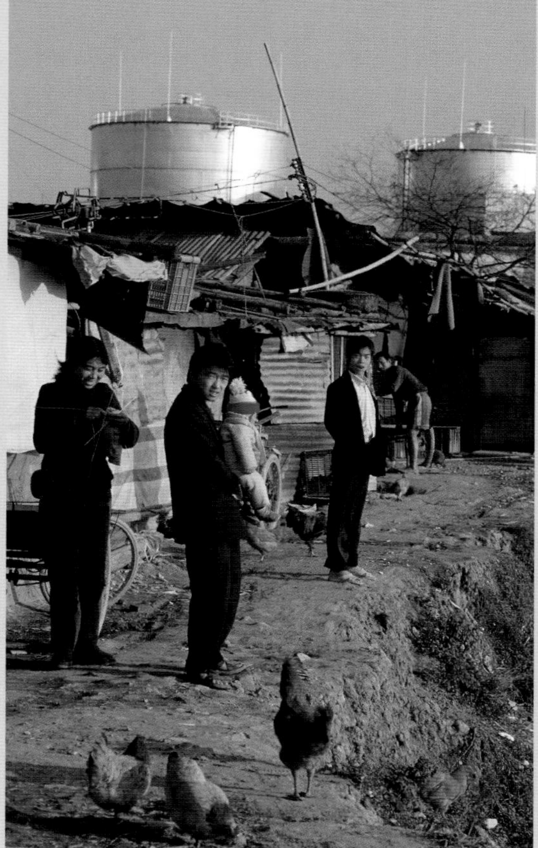

Delta population
Above
Transport infrastructure in the Pearl River Delta region.

Right
Farms and industry as well as humans and chickens coexist on the same plot of land.

rubbish, what is structure and what is not. The land and the water's edge may not be clearly defined, allowing the possibility for accretion in either direction. Landscape on water, water on land. Where does the built environment exist?

2 Delta Population

Asset 2 – Delta Settlements

A potential amphibian land, a delta is neither neutral nor stable. With a rich agricultural soil, it offers an ideal location for dense human settlements. Populations started to occupy places at water intersections and along natural navigation routes, amongst the hills and on higher ground. Amalgamations of villages and towns were determined by community needs when the natural rate of population growth justified them. All such amalgamations were principally administrative; they did not require a new urban plan. With respect to economic reform, formerly separate villages and towns merged together to form a continuous 'built-up' area along new infrastructural corridors.

Guangdong's population is bound to the same regional strength, a place traditionally open to foreign exchange and non-Chinese trade. The majority of the overseas Chinese population originates from this region and has progressively built a powerful and strategic network to expand this system abroad.

Above
Life under the highway
Under the highway, there is a place where one can take a chair, order food and watch TV. This is not only about selling commodities but also encouraging the masses to consume them.

Study 2 – Clan

Rural enterprises are an essential part of economic and urban development within the delta. Today there are plenty of small communities experiencing stronger economic growth than the larger cities. Some villages specialise in producing refrigeration equipment, some in air conditioning and others in umbrellas. This monoproductive culture is derived from 19th-century systems of agroproduction and an interdependence between villages.

Instead of encouraging diversification, economic reform resulted in the hyperspecialisation of each unit and the move towards producing industrialised goods. Capitalising on their strategic location and the demand for land on which to build factories, villages became the richest sources of the delta. As familial responsibility replaced a collective task force, land was divided and part of the production sold on the free market. Solidarity was abandoned for familial profit. A new type of enterprise was created – one where materials, knowledge and machines are imported and assembled in one place to be manufactured and exported. Today, when a village comprises 2,000 official residents, there is a floating population of 60,000 making it work.

Outline 2 - Floating Population

What is the actual population of the PRD? How to sort who is local, who is floating? In Shenzhen, the number of migrant workers supposedly exceeds the local labour force. What does this mean? How to map these cultural fluctuations when space is conceived as a set of relations constituted through social action? Clearly this extensive migrant network illustrates local, translocal and transregional movements as the major characteristics of urban development in south China. Villages from further provinces are broken up, workers are disconnected from urban centres yet they reconnect and re-form their original networks around the factory's locale. This hidden urbanity, which lives off the energy of a population with an average age of 22, represents the necessary motor that powers the region.

3 Delta Economy

Asset 3 – Delta Production

Production networks in the PRD are not recent. Since 1830 the topographic division of the territory has given birth to a complex mosaic of land, each with specific production values. This division is the result of a massive exodus absorbed by the various possibilities of agricultural commerce. Industries such as fishing and silkworm harvesting have evolved through symbiosis – mulberry trees provide a home to the silkworm while their falling leaves are a source of food to fish in surrounding ponds.

Above, top to bottom
Life under the highway
A number of entertainment islands are created by gathering a few chairs or folding a piece of fabric. The highway provides a roof, support for lighting and electricity.

Above and below
Floating population
Dormitories are annexed to the factories. These are six- to eight-storey buildings with rooms for eight women (in most cases) each, along corridors or railed balconies with one bathroom per room and a large balcony for airing clothes.

It is very natural that these small villages developed from an agricultural production to an industrialised economy. The multiplication of rural enterprises, small towns and transport infrastructure are the main determinants of today's organisation. This transition not only involved farming activity but also the size of plots and accessibility to water. This also extends to the erasure of surrounding peaks to fill ponds and create artificial planes that accommodate a growing infrastructure and urban settlements.

Study 3 – Reform
Introduced in 1978, the 'socialist market economy' and 'open door' policy succeeded in transforming the economy; quiet villages were absorbed into a full-blown mega-urban area. As a catalyst to this transformation, the Special Economic Zones (SEZs) of Shenzhen and Zhuhai function like two experimental urban sponges for Hong Kong and Macau. Giving reality to the strategic concept of a 'window', the special zones reflect the image of ongoing reforms. They provide an experimental field to test China's openness to the world, which began by shortening the distance between inland areas and Hong Kong's international markets.

Since the early 1980s, Hong Kong firms have relocated their factories, transforming first Shenzhen then further areas of the PRD, to create a vast manufacturing hinterland. This shift ranges from subcontracted production on behalf of large brand-owning firms in the USA, Europe or Japan, to a domestic consumer market for locally branded goods.

Outline 3 – Made in China
How to scale the production of the capitalist economy? How to combine technology and continuous manpower flow? Endless chains of assembly lines move the world's merchandise. Millions of pairs of hands accelerate this movement. It never stops. Workers make a pause but machinery carries on. Stock is continuously replenished. Waste is recycled on other lines. Clients come back for more. 'Made in China' is sewed into clothes, stitched on shoes, printed on books, stamped on electronics and engraved on furniture. Labels with poor added value for the last 10 years are now becoming high-end products with the latest technology of production and skilled workers. MiC is the largest brand in the world.

4 Lean Production
Asset 4 - Craft and Mass Production
When Henry Ford implemented the first moving assembly line in spring 1913, it marked the end of the craft era. The production of the Ford T in Detroit was completely different from that of the traditional car-maker. Based on a very high level of standardisation in components and connections between elements,

Above
Lean production
A Pandora's box, the factory is a mute block from the outside. Only its logo or name on the facade inform the nature of the production here.

Lean planning is attacking the boundaries that articulate urban space. The contour lines of architecture are fading, and the distinction between centre and periphery, interior and exterior, public and private are disappearing. Instead, a multilayered space of flow encourages a multiplicity of archipelagos that are connected by an efficient networked society under permanent control.

Ford established the basis of mass production. This move coincided with the introduction of new technology and machinery but also with the development of scientific management introduced by the engineer Frederick Winslow Taylor in 1880. Taylorism was based on efficiency and control of every single aspect of production. Through the vertical integration of the factory, and the separation of production and distribution, Ford was literally pushing the product directly into the shops. Modern architecture and city planning were largely inspired by this rationalisation of mass production.

Study 4 – Lean Production

The second move, or revolution, started with the crisis affecting Japanese industrial production after the Second World War. It took from 1949 to 1970 for car producers Eiji Toyoda and Taiichi Ohno to create the concept of lean production, known as the Toyota Production System. The just-in-time manufacturing approach was based essentially on waste reduction. Other aspects such as cost reduction, quality control and maximum flexibility differed radically from mass production. Maximising flow, eliminating waste and adding value to the product and workers are the prerequisites. No stock, no inventory, customisation of product, continuous improvement, flexible and interchangeable operations assure the success and superiority of the Japanese car-maker. The spatial organisation of lean production relies on a stable network of suppliers, small units of production which apply the same technique and become part of the family. Clusters and networks assure smooth production.

Outline 4 – Lean Planning

How to map the unstable environment? How to respond to the most evanescent social phenomena? How to react to 'Made in China'?

Lean planning is attacking the boundaries that articulate urban space. The contour lines of architecture are fading, and the distinction between centre and periphery, interior and exterior, public and private are disappearing. Instead, a multilayered space of flow encourages a multiplicity of archipelagos that are connected by an efficient networked society under permanent control. This control appears at every level and infiltrates the production process as a continual effort collectively managed. Operating at a global scale with decentralised units of production, lean planning expresses a dynamic specific to the delta region.

Conclusion: Lean Planning

Cycles of production and systems of distribution have over the centuries always been an emulator for shaping human settlement. A strategic approach and politics of laissez faire adopted by PRD local-government bodies and then implemented by planners, architects and developers, are in a sense the most up-to-date form of planning. The region has crystallised into a single urban entity based on the opportunistic adoption of an efficient transport infrastructure built with private money to serve the well-distributed factory. With no particular concern for spatial sequence or articulation, these extensive flow lines constitute an effective strategy for colonisation, transforming the landscape into a series of polynuclear construction systems, therefore reinforcing the hybrid condition of the territory.

Within this configuration, access becomes a measure of the mobility and fluidity of urban expansion. In effect, these developments provide the necessary dynamics for a successfully competitive centre that is able to extend its influence into the territory. ⌂

Notes

1 Manuel Castells, *The Rise of the Network Society*, Blackwell (Oxford, UK and Cambridge, US), 1996, p 439.

2 Rem Koolhaas, 'City of exacerbated difference', in Chuihua Judy Chung, Jeffery Inaba, Rem Koolhaas and Sze Tsung Leong (eds) *Great Leap Forward*, Taschen (Cologne), 2001, p 27.

Bangkok: Liquid Perception

'Tropical Bangkok melts familiar epidermal boundaries and extends prior limits of muscular pliancy.' For **Brian McGrath**, the changing physical states that are experienced in Bangkok's intensive tropical climate become a metaphor and simile for the physical, cultural and economic state of the city.

Opposite
Chao Phraya River at the Rama IX Bridge.

Above
The Bangna/Chonburi expressway. A dramatically balanced concrete shading device for the hundreds of thousands of cars that daily use the eight lanes of traffic below.

Changing States

The plane touches down along the fairways of the Royal Thai Air Force golf course between the arced stroke of a tee-off and a shuddering coconut palm. Overbooked Bangkok International Airport discharges passengers on to a steamy, remote tarmac as baggage handlers silently watch from low grasshopper-like squatting positions, their limbs elastic sinews. Foreigners sense a molecular change at the moment of disembarkment as the thick air blankets them with a hot embrace: tropical Bangkok melts familiar epidermal boundaries and extends prior limits of muscular pliancy.

White reflective heat draws the last vapours from exposed patches of earth and human skin. As the temperature approaches 40°C, the city generates its own local thunderstorms, but the pelting rain immediately evaporates upon hitting the fiery tarmac. The concrete city's daily afterglow emits heat until the early morning hours, when fresh gulf breezes finally snake through its waterways and cool ground-water filters up through hidden vegetated pockets, gently misting the waking megalopolis.

International arrival in Bangkok alerts an embodied sense of changing states: instead of the North's familiar cycles of freeze and thaw, here one adjusts to annual and daily cycles of heat-and-moisture exchange. A hardened gaze will crack in the heat of Bangkok, where absorbing, dissolving and evaporating cognition promises 'a more delicate and vaster perception, a molecular perception, peculiar to a cine-eye'.[1]

Absorbing

Climbing the tiered *chedi* (stupa) at Wat Arun, the Temple of Dawn, a Buddhist pilgrim ascends various levels populated with demonic porcelain figures: human, animal, terrestrial and winged. Bangkok's royal temple and palace compounds are constructed as symbolic and physical transcriptions of the Triphumikata, the 14th-century Thai Theravada Buddhist cosmological canon.

The Triphumikata positions reborn souls within 34 karmic levels of existence based on merit and demerit delimited into three worlds: one formless, one free from sensuality, and the familiar realm of form and sense.[2] Thai Buddhist social order employs this world-view to synthesise vastly different forms of knowledge and practices. Cities here are ecumenical and tolerant, heterogeneous and cosmopolitan, populated with a vast diversity of ghostly and living creatures within heavenly and hellish realms, and all that lies in-between. This polystructured and complexly layered ecology historically accommodated Bodhisattvas, spirits and gods of Buddhism, Animism and Brahmanism as well as traders and missionaries from Japan to Holland.

The Thai layered cosmos is not just a description of the world, but of a belief in the simultaneity of material and immaterial existence on different planes. Like cinematic perception that observes an observer through a semisubjective camera eye, Buddhist consciousness is both in the first person, immersed in the sensory world, and located in an objective eye that surveys neutrally from another vantage point. In his two cinema books, Deleuze presents the development of cinema as an intricate semiotic, a cosmology of images and signs, which mirrors the development of contemporary consciousness. Technologically developing cultures

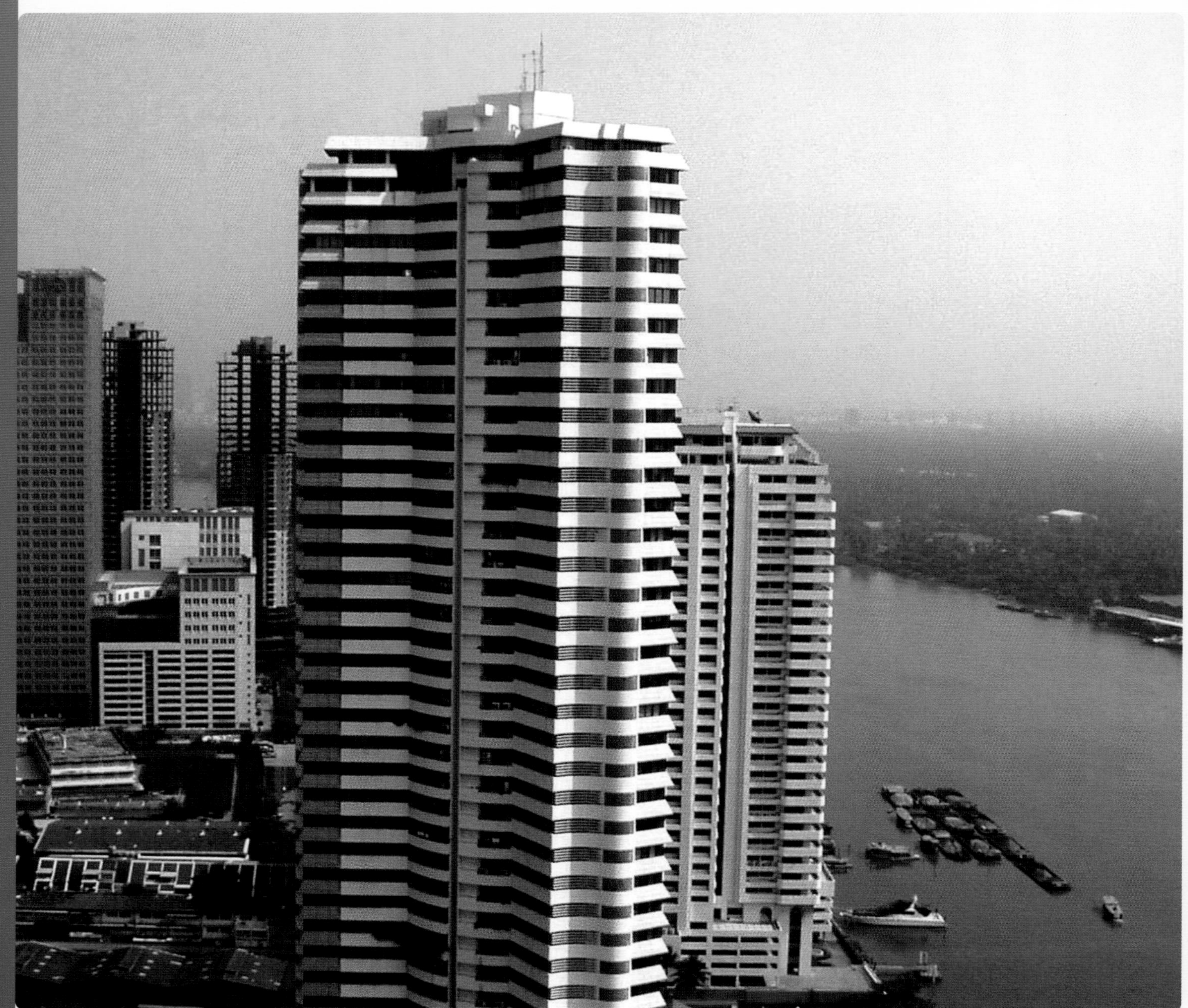

Above
Rama III Road: the new central business district. Hong Kong-style condominium developments line the Chao Phraya River overlooking the fruit orchards of Ban Krachao.

come to terms with becoming modern through cinematic consciousness – full of false continuity, aberrant movement, disproportion of scales, dissipation of centres – calling into question the status of 'normal' movement and measured time. According to Deleuze, in modern cinema the sensory-motor schemata is no longer operative, perceptions and actions cease to be linked, space is neither coordinated nor filled, and characters are caught in pure optical and sound situations – in the sensuality of everydayness itself.[3]

The accommodating Triphumikata cosmology mixes with an emerging Modernist consciousness in contemporary Bangkok at multiple scales and sites. Golf, sex, spa, eco-, agro-, extreme, survival, shopping, health and meditation tours attract not only Westerners but East Asian business and pleasure travellers as well. Confined by a Confucian work ethic at home, they look for refuge and a lost sense of 'Asia-ness' in self-exoticising Thailand. But Bangkok is not just a tourist centre or pleasure zone; it is the economic engine of a newly industrialised economy, a regional business centre for trade, industry and finance, and a magnet for millions of rural migrants in search of employment.

Redundant transit systems operate separate networks for every income and social level. A superimposed matrix of state-sponsored and complexly financed mega-expressway projects and the BTS Skytrain soar above the microcosms of temple and palace enclaves. Ground dwellers slither through traffic along the insufficient metropolitan road system and innumerable informal *sois*, or lanes, while a still-vibrant canal- and river-water-based system provides a more languid journey within a lush yet retreating matrix of canal-fed tropical fruit orchards and rice paddies. This multimodal network converges at the new social incubators and cosmological microcosms of Bangkok: its multilevel shopping malls. The new BTS Skytrain links, and within its stations flat plasma screens advertise, malls, stores and products, forming one of the largest interconnected shopping

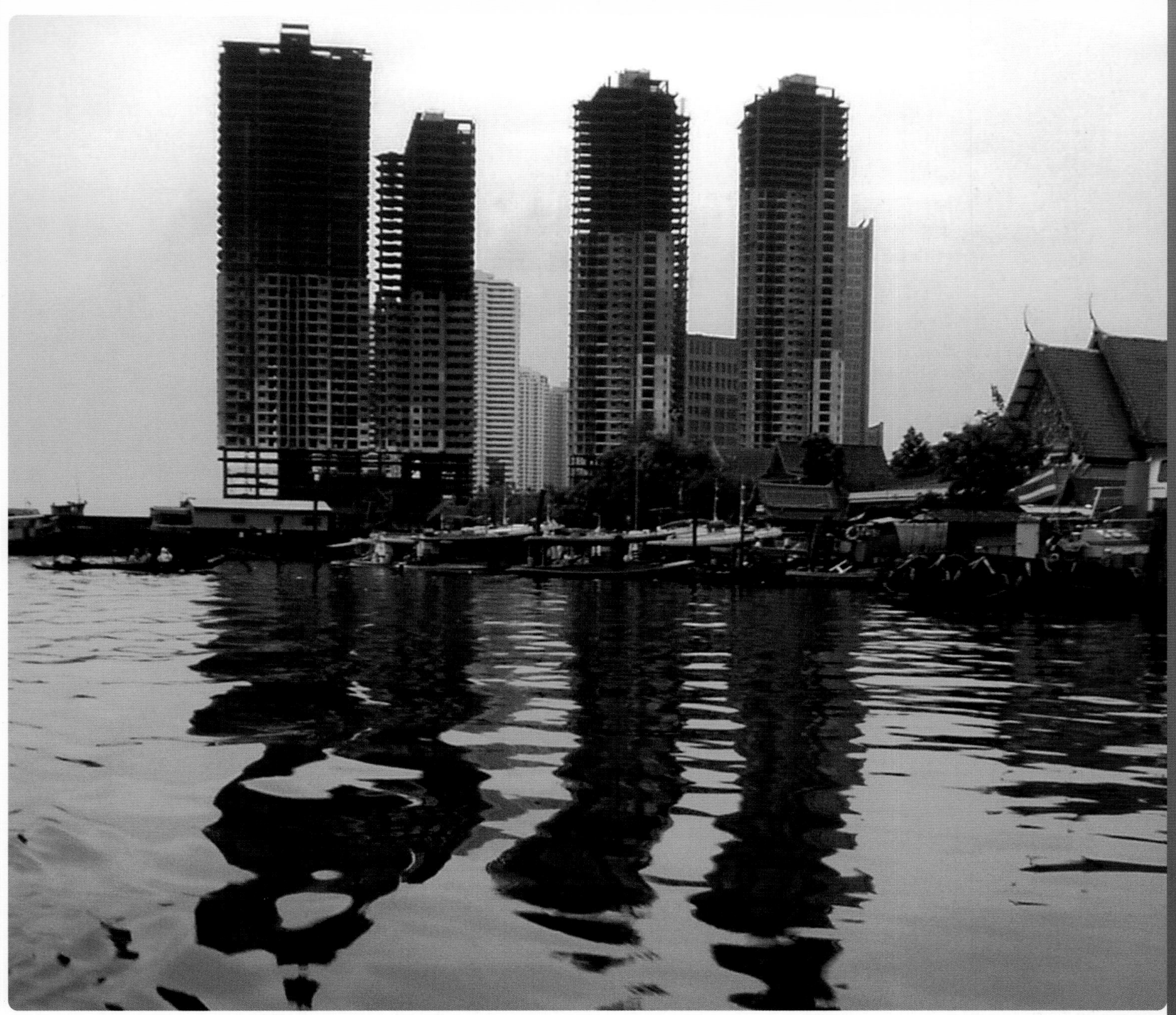

Above
Remnants of the 1997 economic crash: unfinished condominium development, Rama III Road.

and multimedia marketing environments in the world. This is the space in which the youth of Thailand at every income level examines, absorbs and performs global images, technologies and ways of life.

While this consumerist frenzy may seem at odds with the Thai ethical self-consciousness, a Buddhist world-view accepts contradiction and misdirection, and values the immaterial as well as the material; it does not preclude the possibility of incorporating the paraphernalia of late capitalism – especially media images – into its world-view and cosmology.

Dissolving

From a slow-moving long-tail boat, the watery tableau of the Bangkok region unfolds from multiple arteries of the Chao Phraya River Delta. The lower delta is a former seabed, and the city resembles a giant starfish, spreading vegetated tentacles along its old canals and streams. A vast carpet of green orchards and blue paddies unfurls from the vantage point of its sinuous meandering river and tributary canals. Modern development, however, has privileged road-building over maintenance of the canal network. The sticky delta soil barely supports the mix of condominiums, office buildings, golf courses and suburban industrial and housing estates planted in former paddies. All compete for water as the city sprawls over the kingdom's most fertile rice fields.

Walking in subsiding Bangkok is a bumpy encounter with unevenly buckling waves of concrete and paving blocks. Roads, walkways and slabs at ground level buckle and sink a few centimetres a year, while columns and highways built on piles remain stable and rise further from the ground. Intermediate steps are inserted between the upright and sinking levels of the city, giving a bodily measure of the slow descent of a great city into the Bight of Thailand. While flooding is increasingly prevalent, a recent mild earthquake generated much new fear and talk: should a strong quake hit, the vibrating clay soil will liquefy, turning Bangkok into a giant soup of flotsam.

Above
A Chinese ancestor shrine faces an unfinished office development, Rama III Road.

Living in Bangkok requires not only sure-footedness but also an obsessive maintenance of building and body surfaces. Concrete buildings annually mould, peel, crack and flake in dramatically alternating mildewy monsoons and hot dry seasons, while giant billboards beckon Bangkokians to shed their skins, advertising whiteners, oils, lotions and exfoliants.

The old craft of mixing finely sifted white lime with sticky sugar-cane juice produces a hardened eggshell plaster surface, reserved for the Department of Fine Arts temple restorations. Multiple coats of natural resin, black lacquer and gold-leaf angels protect and decorate wood shutters. Inlaid mother-of-pearl, glass or porcelain meticulously decorate doorways and pediments with an assortment of mythical beasts. The legendary *naga* serpent slithers down temple eaves cajoling monsoon rains to flood the paddies. This overabundance of reflective surface decoration dissolves the mass of the buildings in the blinding white sunlight.

In contrast to the heavy maintenance of the masterpieces and Thai high art, the kingdom's simple rural architecture is annually rebuilt from materials harvested around the house – bamboo, giant leaves, grass, rattan and cane. Bangkok's commercial buildings similarly reharvest their surface images. New marble and granite commercial buildings are recast in millennium metallic silver panels and seasonal shopping themes are cause for frequent redecorations. Each holiday event creates the opportunity to remake facades, interior atria, exterior plazas and road medians, while logos cover Bangkok's shopping centres, office buildings, hotels, homes and factories with branded tattoos; a seasonal secular reconstruction of the Triphumikata cosmology.

Evaporating

Thai architecture developed a thermodynamic and social logic before the extravagance of central air-conditioning induced a climatic and cultural amnesia. Before reinforced concrete construction and Corbusier's five points, Thais developed a piloti system

Above
BTS Skytrain at the Siam Discovery Center, Pathumwan intersection.

of posts and beams supporting elaborate umbrella-like roofs shading clustered pavilions surrounding raised exterior living platforms along rivers and canals. This is an elevated architecture of flexibility and grace, unencumbered by heavy furniture, cooled by evaporating watery gardens and inducing a leisurely, almost floating life style. Interior and exterior blend into overlapping zones, but distinctions between shade and sunlight dominate social behaviour.

The programme of the Thai house is not just a private retreat, but an economic space that accommodates multiple activities and flexible, extended family structures. Thai domesticity invades the public realm of Bangkok as straw mats are spread, jasmine garlands are woven or a kitchen is unpacked on the pavement. Wandering the small lanes and alleys of Bangkok is like walking into a variety of crowded, outdoor living-rooms for a wildly diverse extended family. If public space is continually privatised, the private realm is open to the street and invitingly public.

Early-modern architects in Bangkok reinvented the international Modernist canon with an indigenous awareness of the interrelations between climate, environment, body, heat regulation and informal social behaviour. Remnants of this confidently crafted, early-modern architecture – and the social life it encourages – persist in schools, universities and government offices, as well as in older hotels and houses. These open and accommodating buildings welcome casual short-cuts. Generous vestibules, terraces, halls, balconies and stairways are all outside; only classrooms or offices are enclosed. Everyday life is constantly interrupted by this generous exterior realm. Work is broken up by changes in weather, vegetation, bird songs, stray dogs and chance encounters.

The more recent embrace of central air-conditioning has accompanied sloppy industrialised building production, and the mistaken belief that global business and tourism demand cheaply finished, hermetically

Bundit Chulasai, the Bundit House, Bangkok, 1999

Above and opposite
Chulasai describes the house he built for himself during the depths of the Thai economic crisis in the late 1990s as a creative and pragmatic response to the cultural context of a newly industrial society. The natural resources that supported the traditional Thai way of life are no longer available, yet the technological, economic and human means of achieving a 'modern' society remain out of reach. His house, therefore, is an economical, practical, modern concrete frame and block house that captures the Thai domestic spirit within. Bundit's colleague at Chulalongkorn University, Professor Piyalada Thoveeprungsriporn, calls this spirit 'rom reun' quality, the cool and refreshing sensation associated with traditional Thai houses, now located six floors above the congested streets of central Bangkok.

sealed, isolating bubbles. As a result, the city that historically developed as porous compounds in a temperature-regulating watery garden has become a constellation of heat-generating and socially segregating islands.

Despite the constant mobility required by a modern metropolis, Bangkok stubbornly retains a slow pace, produces the most aberrant of movements and induces countless sedentary breaks from activity. The climate and the culture dictate release from constant 'doing', and tempt the art of just sitting or reclining and doing nothing but watching and listening to the city.

According to Deleuze, liquid perception evaporates into a gaseous state when cinematic movement is no longer associated with action but reverses, slows down or stops our view of the world. During the booming economy before 1997, Bangkokians seemed to have lost sight of the benefits of this state of being in a mad rush towards development. After hundreds of millions of dollars evaporated overnight, post-bubble societal soul-searching has produced a desire to recover those qualities of the city that are most valuable to both its citizens and visitors alike.

A remarkable example of this yearning is the home architect Bundit Chulasai designed for himself in Bangkok: an outdoor living-room suspended on the seventh floor between concrete piers. The floating living-room is framed by the building's cores: kitchen and library to the north, bathroom, lift and stairs to the south, while the bedroom soars above. As recycled waste-water feeds a generous assortment of potted plants, planes land at five-minute intervals on the horizon and guests can survey the more than 300 unfinished skyscraper skeletons that form Bangkok's skyline. Both a meditative retreat and cinematic frame for the city around, Bundit's house is a model for modern, high-density mid-rise housing incorporating the logic of outdoor tropical life style for a society that privileges leisurely, playful and open social contact over individual privacy.

Notes
1 Gilles Deleuze, *Cinema 1: The Movement Image*, Minnesota University Press (Minneapolis), 1986, p 80.
2 Pinraj Khanjanusthiti, 'Buddhist Architecture: Meaning and Conservation in the Context of Thailand', PhD thesis, University of York, 1996.
3 Gilles Deleuze, *Cinema 2: The Movement Image*, Minnesota University Press (Minneapolis), 1988, p 37.
4 Peter A Jackson, *Buddhadasa: Theravada Buddhism and Modernist Reform in Thailand*, Silkworm Books (Chiang Mai), 2003.
5 The author would like to thank Dean Vira Sachakul and the Faculty of Architecture at Chulalongkorn University.

Changing States of Capitalism

As capitalism changes states it is urgent to develop new tools to perceive the changing state of capitalism. Our image of Asian urbanism and late 20th-century globalisation is formed by Japan, Taiwan, South Korea, Hong Kong and Singapore: insular, Confucian cultures that developed highly uniform, self-sacrificing, apartment-dwelling, educated, middle-class, urban, industrial societies within a generation.

The 1997 Asian financial crisis demonstrated that this economic model could not be sustained, and the young from Seoul to Singapore seem no longer willing to make the same sacrifices as their parents. Bangkok's liquid, horizontal space of pure decentralised potentiality – where extreme social possibilities emerge at any point in the city – appeals to the restless tastes of this new generation and represents a new wave of Asian urbanism. Rampant unpredictability coexists in Thailand along with the embodied certainty guaranteed by the Theravada cosmology under the symbolic leadership of a Dhamma king and the political guidance of a telecommunications-billionaire prime minister. In fact, contemporary radical Buddhism reinterprets the Triphumikata's representational levels of heaven, hell, demons and gods, not as a literal description of the universe but as a metaphorical explanation for changing psychological states, altered states of consciousness and keener perceptions here and now.[4]

Cities reform our world-view and create embodied knowledge. Contemporary cinema helps us find our way in a non-narrative, fluid, decentred and atemporal urban world. Following Henri Lefebvre's call for the regeneration of the city commencing with a restoration of the body, radical Buddhist Bangkok's absorbing, dissolving and evaporating urban consciousness promises a keener recognition of the relations between the world, our desires and ourselves as subjects and producers of urban capital's complex flows of energy and matter.[5] ⌂

Recon-struction Solidarity: The Thao Tribe

Like many grass-roots makeshift responses to the urban condition in Asia, the low-cost self-build housing solution that Ying Chun Hsieh has created for the Thao tribe in central Taiwan represents a local resistance or ambivalence to globalism. As **Nicholas Boyarsky** explains, this is a position that has not gone unnoticed by those with a capital interest in construction in the area, who have felt that Hsieh is cutting them out of a lucrative market. Hsieh's personal safety has been under threat on several occasions.

Opposite
The Thao tribe has the smallest population of all the aboriginal tribes in Taiwan: 281. Despite its small size it has retained its own unique customs, culture, language and ancestral beliefs and rituals. Most of the tribe's members live in Brawbaw on the banks of the Sun Moon Lake in central Taiwan. The massive earthquake that shook Taiwan in September 1999 damaged or destroyed 80 per cent of the Thao tribe's houses.

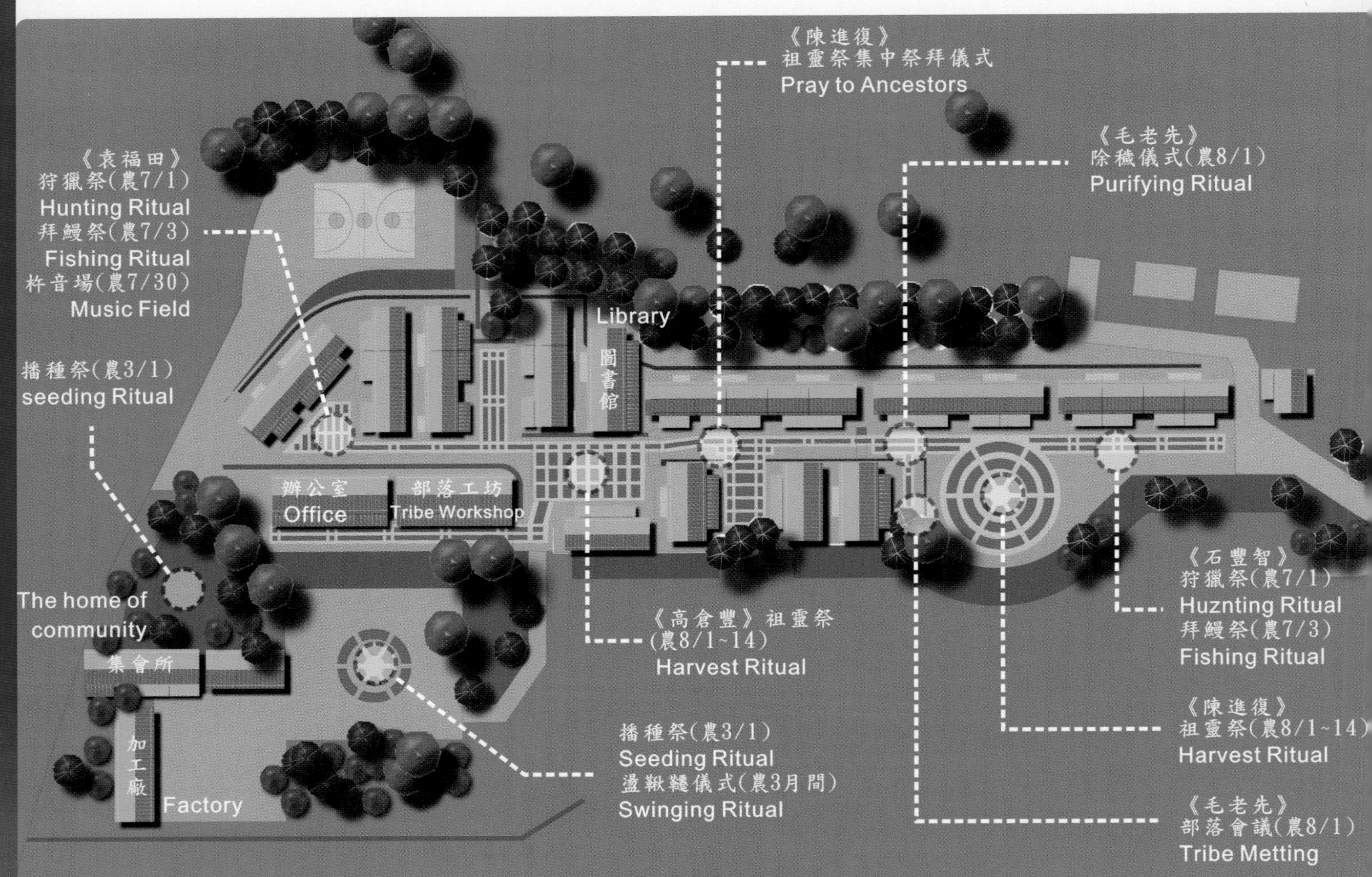

Above
Building the village. Further encroachment of the concept of private property and commercialisation has completely undermined the original system of communal ownership of the tribe and separated the symbiotic links between its members.

Ying Chun Hsieh heads a group of young architects in the 921 Disaster Area Housing Reconstruction Service Group who live and work at Sun Moon Lake, Taiwan. He is currently developing modular housing elements that can be used for putting up a house for a cost of between NT$220,000 and NT$900,000 – about half conventional construction costs.

Hsieh's concept is based on the social role that architecture can play. One of the most important aspects of his project is the simplification of the construction. 'Complex construction methods require the use of skilled workers imported from outside. By simplifying construction, the aborigines can build the houses themselves.' The implications of this go far beyond DIY. 'It is really about the exchange of labour. By bringing in friends and family, working weekends and so forth, the cost of the house can be further reduced.'

Working from his camp in the Thao Community, Hsieh has set up a simple factory where the modular elements of the buildings are made. Most of the complex design work has already been done, and components simply have to be bolted together. Provision is even made for the hanging of scaffolding, to increase safety for the workers, many of whom are drawn from the ranks of the unemployed in the area. With Hsieh's modular elements, simple power tools and a truck hoist, a two-storey house can be put together within a day.

'The Thao tribe has the smallest population of all the aboriginal tribes in Taiwan: 281. Despite its small size it has retained its own unique customs, culture, language and ancestral beliefs and rituals. Most of the tribe's members live in Brawbaw on the banks of the Sun Moon Lake in central Taiwan. The massive earthquake that shook Taiwan in September 1999 damaged or destroyed 80 per cent of the Thao tribe's houses.

Because of the Taiwanese government's past mistakes in policy, the Thao's land was not incorporated as land reserved for aborigines. As a result, most of the land has been expropriated or cheated away by Han Chinese and the government, leaving the originals with no land to plant crops. The tribe is skilled at fishing, but is unable to compete with the developed marketing of the Chinese. Most of the members of the tribe now work as menial workers, cooks and vendors in the tourist industry at Sun Moon Lake.

The elder system is not very marked in Thao society. Public affairs of the tribe, particularly rituals, are handled during tribal meetings and carried out by different clans and clan elders.

Community Layout Based Around Ritual Space

After Brawbaw was incorporated by the state in Taiwan, nearly all of the Thao tribe's ritual spaces (open areas for drying grain) were forcibly purchased by the government and given to public officials or Han Chinese. The tribe was forced to hold its rituals in the middle of roads.

Above
Working from his camp in the Tehua Community, Hsieh has set up a simple factory where the modular elements of the buildings are made. Most of the complex design work has already been done, and components simply have to be bolted together. With Hsieh's modular elements, simple power tools and a truck hoist, a two-storey house can be put together within a day.

While rituals are under way the tribe places two bamboo poles to signify the scope of the ritual area, and people and animals are forbidden from entering. While simple in appearance, the ritual space is very solemn and filled with taboos. This seriousness is not possible if the rituals take place on the road where cars and people are constantly passing through.

Community Consciousness Based on Collective Work

Members of the Thao tribe account for only 20 per cent of the population in Brawbaw. Moreover, through changes to land zoning laws the government has broken up the holdings of the tribe in the community. Further encroachment of the concept of private property and commercialisation has completely undermined the original system of communal ownership of the tribe and separated the symbiotic links between its members.

The earthquake led to the collective unemployment of the Thao tribe. Many tribe members were able to collect money from the government by carrying out reconstruction work, which also allowed them to rebuild a sense of a shared community through shared work. Rebuilding housing requires a great deal of coordinated labour, and links between members of the tribe were re-established through the process. This should serve as a future base for even closer relations among the tribe.

Wages account for about half the cost of constructing a building. If the government hopes that earthquake victims can construct their own houses to help alleviate the unemployment problem, then simple designs and construction methods must be devised to allow people not skilled in construction – including housewives and the elderly – to take part in the reconstruction efforts.

One such type of building is constructed out of a lightweight steel frame, with thin steel plates held together by easily installed screws thereby avoiding welding. The structure is easy to construct, safe, and can be taken apart and put up with a power screwdriver. Installation of windows, beds and showers is also simple. The roof of the structure is made of plywood, oilcloth and bamboo, which is virtually free for the picking in the mountains. Roofs and walls constructed from bamboo are easy to build and to replace if they rot. Bamboo roofs are constructed with two layers that allow air to flow in-between, dispersing heat from the hot sun beating down on the roof. Long eaves also provide shade, while screens keep out insects but still provide a clear view of the sky as well as ventilation to the house. Steel is another reusable resource, and the ease with which the buildings can be put up and taken down makes for straightforward reconstruction.

Aboriginal houses do not have separate bedrooms, but bamboo strips instead. Outer walls are constructed out of bamboo strips with an inner layer of aluminium insulation or cloth for heat insulation that also keeps out water and insects. Δ

to incise
to enable
to cut
to fragment

to coexist
to connect
to activate
to collaborate

to protest
to self-organise
to irritate
to engage

to pause
to juxtapose
to troubleshoot
to include

Action (Verb) Taipei

Here, **Sand Helsel**, 'an Asian architect' born in the US and teaching at RMIT in Melbourne, and also actively involved in conferences, workshops and study tours in Taiwan, Korea, Hong Kong, Indonesia and Malaysia, provides insights into Taipei through extracts from her urban diary.

The verb list provides a counterpoint to the adjectives normally applied to the Asian city – words such as 'dense', 'rapidly developing', 'chaotic' and 'ad hoc'. Unlike these general descriptions contributed by Western urbanists, the verbs are from (and about) people making, working and being in the region. This is not a language of hyperbolic qualifiers: extra-large or mega-Dutch. It is not about the imposition of a formalist overlay from above or afar. A different scale of operation and an intimate connection with the material at hand – the city – is implied, in the way that a sculptor such as Richard Serra might work. 'To master-plan' makes a rather clumsy verb in this context.

The plan of Taipei produced by the Department of Urban Design (see opposite) is an extraordinary document. Building lines and city blocks are delineated; city streets and pavements are drawn. However, this is where convention stops. Only the hatched buildings exist legally, with approvals from the statutory authorities and in accordance with the master plan. All crosshatched structures are illegal in this context, and have been constructed according to the rules of some other system. Lanes are filled in, or become internal courtyards; the pavement disappears at times. New typologies are created: arcade insertions, donut buildings, wrap-around commerce. Any open bit of land appears up for grabs. The authority that the map might have is challenged by the entrepreneurship of the inhabitants. This is considered a viable alternative to the systems of legislation and planning prevalent in most Western cities. A form of *civitas* in action.

Urban Diary[1]

I fell in love with Taipei after my first visit. How does one operate when taking students to Taipei? I realised that this dilemma became a paradigm for how one might operate in the Asian city. While it is often considered a problem to work outside one's cultural milieu, for fear of a lack of understanding, of misreading, we use this as an opportunity for discourse. The work strives to find common pleasures within the city and to accommodate different readings – what some regard as strengths, others may consider weaknesses. The seemingly banal is reconsidered. This dialogue becomes a paradigm for the city; the issue is that of negotiation, to allow for the different voices to be heard and for multiple narratives and complexity. The architect can assist in this act of curation. One becomes a sort of Taipei operationist providing an alternative model for examination, speculation and proposition that is based on an intimate connection to the city.

Urban Diary[2]

'The World Famous Mango Ice Store'; operative verb: to negotiate. A 24-hour 'stakeout' reveals not only an entrepreneurial spirit in the (illegal) appropriation of the public space of the street, but also a social code in the system of negotiation with adjacent businesses.

The structure opens at 11am and begins to gradually unfold on to the adjacent lot and footpath: tables and chairs, service stations, overflow from the kitchen. The popularity of this fruit-and-ice treat grows throughout the day; the crowds build, illegally parked cars and service vehicles expand the 'building's' perimeter deep into the neighbourhood. By 6pm an employee from the ice store arrives to establish an unobstructed frontage to the Japanese restaurant next door when the queues get long.

to loosely connect	to graft	to find	to deregulate
to incorporate	to choose	(hidden orders)	to understand
to maintain memory	to adapt	to find	to misunderstand
to overlap	to pose questions	(common ground)	to negotiate

Urban Diary[3]
The garbage truck arrives at 8pm on Monday nights playing a digitised version of Mozart's *A Little Night Music*. The neighbourhood gathers with its assortment of rubbish.

Through critique, the observations of the existing conditions are evaluated for their strengths and weaknesses, and the opportunities they offer and the threats they pose. All opinions are acknowledged and respected. In some instances a phenomenon can be considered both positively and negatively. I, personally, remain charmed by the garbage and recycling truck that arrived in my neighbourhood on a Monday evening heralding its arrival with a blasting digital version of Mozart's *A Little Night Music*; the neighbourhood congregates to personally load its rubbish in an event that felt like a gathering in a village square.

The authors of an alternative proposal to rubbish collection in the Hong Kong district are less romantic than myself, realising that this 'ritual' poses a nuisance to those with large families, during a monsoon, and for the elderly or handicapped. Through an awareness of the range of possible interpretations they pose questions that avoid an oversimplification of the problem(s), and thus a subsequent expedient response. Their strategy to create neighbourhood recycling centres maintains the community spirit and ensures a continued economic mix, the reuse of abandoned historic Japanese houses, the continued relevance of urban typologies such as the shop house and the light-industrial unit in the face of impending high-rise development, and an alternative system of navigation within the urban fabric in addition to a viable environmental proposal. By being able to deal with the complexity of the site phenomena, they create a true sustainable project with its requisite breadth of concerns.

Urban Diary: A Conclusion

Although the work is particular to Taipei, the process of observation and mapping reveals phenomena that have currency for other cities and design practice in general. These celebrations of the rituals and ordinariness of daily life, the exploration of the hidden systems that shape the city, and the particularities of speed, mobility and density and their physical implications, all contribute to a reading of Taipei that also has resonance with issues that affect other urban centres, regardless of scale and locale.

Our traditional spheres of operation as architects, at 1:200 scale in plan and section, for instance, are of little use to us when contending with a highway or grasping with issues such as the sustainable agenda. When working at a larger scale we are often distanced from our subject matter and create the sort of disenfranchisement that is addressed by 'urban agitators' like the Situationists in Paris and the Stalker Group in Italy. I concur that it is our responsibility to enable and empower our constituents in the curation of the city. Δ

Above
Excerpt from the plan of Taipei produced by the Department of Urban Design. Only the hatched buildings are legal, all cross-hatched structures are illegal.

Notes
1 From notes taken by Sand Helsel during the presentations and discussions of the conference proceedings 'How Small is the City', Urban Flashes 2, Linz, Austria, April 2002.
2 The verb list is homage to Richard Serra's 'Verb List' in Gregoire Muller, *The New Avant-Garde: Issues for the Art of the Seventies*, Praeger (New York), 1972, p 94.
3 From Peter Ryan, 'The World Famous Mango Ice Store', in 'Taipei Operations', exhibition and forthcoming book, curated and edited by Sand Helsel and KC Bee.

Modern Heritage: A Terrain of the Question

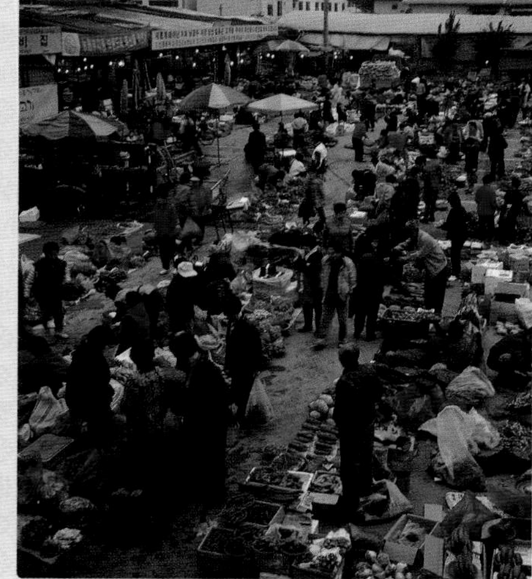

Guyon Chung describes how a redundant railway line in Gwangiu, a core town in southwest Korea, has created a natural caesura in the continual growth and flow of the city. Popular public consensus demanded that the slither of land not be redeveloped but greened with a dense planting of trees. This has not only markedly improved the quality of life of Gwangiu's inhabitants but has also allowed a sense of community to evolve out of an urban void.

Opposite
Aerial view of Project4 on abandoned station site. Land has its inherent meanings and attributes according to its specific location. In order to induce reflections on the importance of the land, simple facilities or temporary structures are inserted with consideration for the surrounding environment.

Above
Nam Gwangiu Market Square. Once a small town with less than 10,000 citizens in the early 20th century, Gwangiu is now a core city in the southwest of the Korean peninsula with a population of over 1.3 million.

Right
Historical view of Gwangiu railway. When a train that ran through the city core for 70 years suddenly ceased operation, resulting in an immediate pause in the use of land that stretches 10.8 kilometres across Gwangiu, the citizens were forced to face an unprecedented situation.

1 Flowing and Pause

The city is like a living organism, constantly moving and changing. Not that it is mobile by nature but, to sustain its urban life, it requires duration and ceaseless reproduction of numerous forms of flows. Maintaining the flow of people, materials, goods, electricity, water (both supply and sewage), gas, voices, signs, wastes, motor vehicles and trains is essential for the city's survival. At times, however, it seems that the city exists to support such a flow – the flow itself is the city's *raison d'être* – rather than the flow supporting the lives of its people. Therefore, when the flow pauses, events occur that provide an occasion to look back upon the city and its flow.

In fear of a blackout, computer-users tend to click the save button every few minutes; when the lights actually go out, candles replace light bulbs. Expecting suspension of supply, water is stored in tubs; and bicycles are used when public transport goes on strike. There have always been substitutes sustaining the city's flow. When a train that ran through the city core for 70 years suddenly ceased operation, resulting in an immediate pause in the use of land that stretches 10.8 kilometres across Gwangiu, the citizens were forced to face an unprecedented situation.

2. Modern Heritage: Time and Space Sealed

Once a small town with less than 10,000 citizens in the early 20th century, Gwangiu is now a core city in the southwest of the Korean peninsula with a population of over 1.3 million. Like other cities in Korea, it has experienced a period of rapid industrialisation for the last 30 years – horizontal expansion necessitated subway networks and resulted in the large-scale construction of satellite towns outside of the old centre. This process of enlargement is not so special, save for the closing of the Gwangryeo line – a railway built back in 1930 that extends 10.8 kilometres across Gwangiu. In more recent times the railway had been accused of having a negative influence on traffic flow and degrading the environment of neighbouring towns.

All of a sudden, the railway in the middle of the city was abandoned, and this *terrain vague* now awaits new connections to the urban fabric. However, the site is not just another public space in a city. When the railway was built the site was situated at the outskirts of Gwangiu. Then the growth of the city skipped over the area, which has now become part of the city core. Like the portion in a child's drawing outlined by a wax candle into which watercolour cannot permeate, it is where the wave of urban sprawl overran, where the development was reserved for another time, and where the trace of time was carved into the city itself. Its sealed time and space, along with the rails and sleepers, is now pulled out – ironically, it looks as though the railway is just about to be built. The land from 70 years back is suddenly overlaid upon the present site. As a result, it has lost its original purpose – it remains a keyhole in a padlock that should be approached by another time and space.

In other words, this abandoned site is not a tabula rasa but a modern heritage of Gwangiu, not simply a void area but a land of potentials interacting with its surroundings, a plane rather than a line, a continuous scenery rather than a railway, inspiring link and connection over boundary and discontinuity, a place of ecological expression and recovering nature beyond the rubble, not a road destined to perish but an open future. It is a terrain of the question which should be reapproached with a comprehensive point of view prior to any form of reuse. It is not common to completely shut down an urban railway.

This abandoned site is not a tabula rasa but a modern heritage of Gwangiu, not simply a void area but a land of potentials interacting with its surroundings, a plane rather than a line, a continuous scenery rather than a railway, inspiring link and connection over boundary and discontinuity, a place of ecological expression and recovering nature beyond the rubble, not a road destined to perish but an open future.

3. Connection: Subject and Reason

It was the citizens who achieved the first connection – as soon as the railway ceased operation their collective wish to have an urban greenway connected with the abandoned site. Until now, momentum for urban change has mostly come from the government authorities who are notorious for hasty decisions and shoddy implementation of urban programmes, however complex the issues concerned. The decisions these bodies make regarding the use of space are always a surprise to the citizens. Though there are sometimes instances when they hold public hearings prior to decision-making, these are strictly formal.

The city government's initial plan for the abandoned railway was to use it as an electric railway, but such an idea was met with great resistance from the people of Gwangiu, and as a result of great public effort a greenway of dense trees was eventually created at the heart of the city instead. The major reason why this incident is significant is that it paved the way for the people to exercise their natural rights to build within the city what they deemed necessary. Its success was the result of unprecedented consensus among the people.

This is the starting point of building a community – a concept that usually seems irrelevant to the realities of contemporary cities. People have now come to think of land not in reductive terms of area or realty, but as a latent energy that can improve their quality of life. The success of the greenway was also due to the fact that the site was empty – it was an example of generating community through an urban void. The voluntary formation of a public value by the people is what we call the creation of culture, and here it is manifested by replacing the road of steel with that of culture, and territorialising the deterritorialised soil for the good of the citizens. However just the will and choices of the citizens may be, the road for its realisation nonetheless varies – the length of 10.8

Above and opposite
Joong+Keun Lee House/ Home: Strawberry & Sunflower. People have now come to think of land not in reductive terms of area or realty, but as a latent energy that can improve their quality of life.

kilometres does not present in a uniform condition and, depending on the overall concept or methodology, the new greenway could be either rich or monotonous in character.

Land Art

Even before the abolishment of the railway, neighbours were using parts of the site to plant vegetables, and cultivated land among the rubble and rail sleepers has since become a refreshing element of the urban landscape.

Open-Air Museum

It is unfortunate that all that is left of the 70-year history of Nam-Gwangiu station is its site. By connecting the railway, the people, Nam-Gwangiu market and the remains of the platform, a half-broken bridge and other vestiges of the railway, a concrete place is constructed that enables people to encounter the history of the past.

Architectural Landscape

Land has its inherent meanings and attributes according to its specific location. In order to induce reflections on the importance of the land, simple facilities or temporary structures are inserted with consideration for the surrounding environment.

Connection

The construction of railways reduced or ruptured the cultural, historical value of the city, but by adding new devices to the present site alleys, bridges and hills next to the railway can be reinvigorated. No longer the city's dividing agent, the rail can now promote harmony through its connection with the previously disconnected.

Nomadic Shelter

Urbanisation, accompanied by the increase of the urban population, naturally leads to a boost in nomadic lives. As a result we now have dynamic cities and mobile homes. These may well reflect the wisdom of urban living, and could help to enrich the assets of the city.

Open-Air Classroom

The adjacent region of the site is for the most part a residential area with a number of educational institutions. The site could be used as an open-air classroom for these schools, offering students the chance to observe the ecosystem of its nature.

Urban Ecology

The traces of botanical life along the disused railway that runs through the city present a clear section of Gwangiu's ecology, and alternative possibilities of the city can be found in its ecological characters, especially those of the railway which, used for 70 years under different conditions, has formed its own peculiar environment.

Promenade and Daily Sports Experience

Artistically rendered facilities or structures for walking or sports could add diversity to the citizens' everyday lives.

Vision

What will the future be like for an ever-changing city and life within it? Aren't the abounding fluids and pollutants (such as noise) of contemporary society and urban spaces actual clues to imagining what is to come? Is the trip to the invisible city beyond our reach? As George Simmel remarked: 'The spiritual aspects of life in the metropolis have incited intellectual rather than emotional response to outer stimuli, which resulted in the proliferation of the abstract in men.'[1] The promotion of private lives in the city stems from the characteristic of modern civilisation that places objectivity over subjectivity. But with the themes introduced above, citizens can learn to correspond to their daily activities and consume part of their city subjectively and emotionally, gaining balance in urban living. Spirit would thus be formed within the city, and the city would condition the spirit of the citizens. ⌂

Note

1 Francoise Choay, *L'Urbanisme, Utopies et Realities: Une Autholoige*, Ed du Seuil (Paris), 1965, p 409.

Hanoi

Above
Cycling feet.

Opposite, top
Real and fake ladies.

Opposite, upper middle right
Courtyard peace.

Opposite, upper middle left
Xe dap (bicycle) repair men.

Opposite, lower middle right
Phone numbers on a wall.

Opposite, lower middle left
Outdoor *cat toc* (haircut) space.

Opposite, bottom left
Dangling rope.

Opposite, bottom right
Hanoi skyline across the Red River.

An urbanist as well as a photographer, **Justine Graham** has a special interest in the boundaries of public and private space. In this project undertaken in Hanoi, Vietnam, she specifically focused on the way that small-scale commercial ventures encroach on the street, competing for attention amid the hustle of everyday city life.

The recent wake of Vietnam's liberalising economic policies, or *Doi Moi*, has produced the boom of a rapidly growing sector of a society previously engaged in state-provided work that now ventures into small, privately owned businesses. This has meant a drastic increase in the use of the street for commercial use and an extended exertion of the built environment. The encroachment on to the street for personal and commercial uses such as pavement stalls, the spilling out of wares from cramped shops and the parking of motorcycles and bicycles is now part of the contemporary Hanoi streetscape.

The sanitised, modern Western city it is not. Hanoi's seamless chaos is noisy, full-on, exhausting, exhilarating and inscribed with daily urban rituals. These repeated gestures involve sweeping one's entrance, exercising in public spaces at 6am, navigating the streets amidst hoards of street vendors and motorbikes, sitting on street corners gossiping around a bowl of *pho* (traditional soup), or simply wandering the dark streets when the evening lights are turned off. Amidst the smell of incense and motorbike fumes, the sounds of squealing pigs off to the market, street vendors announcing their goods, and the interminable sight of plastic and crafted objects for sale, I looked for quieter signs of human presence: a dangling rope on a construction site, a peaceful courtyard, an outdoor haircut shop, phone numbers on a wall. ◭

REVLON
THỜI TRANG U.S.A
HẰNG
TEL: 263047

CĂN VÀNH
XE MÁY

CẮT TÓC

8528259
8287874
7.53041

Sue Barr is a photographer and tutor at the Architectural Association in London. She travelled to Japan to photograph Gaikoku Mura in the summer of 2002, work that along with an accompanying essay by Japanese architect and critic Akira Suzuki was exhibited at the AA in January 2003. Current exhibition projects include an exploration into the demarcations of architectural 'non-space' (the gaps between recognised places) and 'The Art of Parking', a historical typology of multistorey car parks. Her work has been featured in numerous international journals and publications.

Nicholas Boyarsky is a London-based architect and educator. He is a director of the award-winning practice Boyarsky Murphy Architects, which he co-founded with Nicola Murphy in 1993. He has taught and lectured internationally and is currently a visiting professor at Bergen Architecture School in Norway. He has been a core member of the Urban Flashes Group from its inception in 1999.

Gary Chang graduated from the Department of Architecture, University of Hong Kong, in 1987, and founded EDGE in 1994. Since 1995 he has been teaching as an associate professor at the Department of Architecture of HKU, and is a lecturer in SPACE HKU. He has also lectured at the Technische Universiteit (Delft), Royal College of Art (London) and Milan Polytechnic. His first solo exhibition was held at the Hong Kong Arts Centre in 2000. He was among the first group of representatives from Hong Kong to be invited to participate in the International Biennial Exhibition of Architecture, Venice, in 2000, and again in 2002.

Ti-Nan Chi is principal of Chi's Workshop & Z Architects, Taipei. In 1999 he founded the Urban Flashes networking and Human Environment Group NGO. He studied at Yale under Frank Gehry and philosopher Karsten Harries. His works have been exhibited at 'Cities on the Move' at Secession/PS1/Hayward Gallery (Vienna/New York/London) in 1997, 'Ker Da Ker Xiao' at the Architectural Association, London, in 1998, 'East Wind' at Park Tower, Tokyo, 2000, and the Venice Biennale at Arsenale, Venice, 2000. Publications include the design document *Tangibleintangible* (1998), *Thinking Architecture* (1992) and *Trans-Prophecy* (1999).

Architect **Guyon Chung** attented the Ecole Nationale Superieure des Arts Decoratifs (1972–5), Unite Pedagogique d'Architecture No 6 (1975–9) and Universite Paris VIII, Institut d'Urbanisme (1979–82). He founded Guyon Architects Associates in 1986. He has been the directive member of Seoul School of Architecture since 1995 and is a professor at the Korean National University of Arts. He has received several honours such as the Architectural & Cultural Contribution Prize from Jinju City (1997) and the Kyobo Environmental and Cultural Award (Architecture, 2000).

Tokyo-born **Nobuyaki Furuya** received his Masters in Architecture from Waseda University, Tokyo, in 1980. From 1986 to 1987 he worked in the studio of Mario Botta, and from 1989 to 1994 was assistant professor at Kinki University. In 1994 he established NASCA in Tokyo, and in 1999 was made professor at Waseda University. Awards include the Japan Institute of Architecture (JIA) Award 2000, 2002 and 2003, and the JIA Annual Award 2003. He is also vice-president of the JIA.

Justine Graham is an urbanist and photographer working in London. She has worked for the Architecture Foundation and General Public Agency as a project coordinator, and is now freelancing for various cultural projects relating to the public realm and urban regeneration. Her photographic work revolves around urban space and the boundaries between public and private spaces, with a strong interest in non-Western cities.

Laurent Gutierrez and **Valérie Portefaix** are French architects living and working (teaching) in Hong Kong. In 1997 they founded MAP Office, a collaborative studio involved in cross-disciplinary projects that incorporate architecture and the visual arts. They have participated in international exhibitions including the 7th Architecture Venice Biennale and the 1st International Architecture Biennale in Rotterdam, where they won an award for the best 'inspiration'. Current research focuses on 'lean planning', which explores the impact of economic production and distribution mapped on to a reconvertible environment, and the specific 'Made in China' conditions of the Pearl River Delta region.

New York-born **Sand Helsel** was educated in London at the Architectural Association, and is Associate Professor of Architecture at RMIT in Melbourne. She has organised and participated in conferences, workshops and study tours in Taiwan, Korea, Hong Kong, Indonesia and Malaysia. Her practice straddles the traditional disciplinary boundaries between art, architecture, landscape, urbanism and engineering. Taipei Operations is a touring exhibition. A book is also in progress.

Hirohisa Hemmi is an associate architect at Kajima Design, Tokyo. He studied with Kazuo Shinohara at Tokyo Institute of Technology where he received his Master of Engineering degree. As a Fulbright scholar he received his Master of Architecture degree from Yale in 1987, and worked for Richard Meier and Partners in Los Angeles before rejoining Kajima Design. Since 1998 he has collaborated with Shinohara on publication projects concerning the city and the house. The first of the series was published as *Discourse on Tokyo from Tokyo, via Kazuo Shinohara*, in 2001.

Ying Chun Hsieh graduated in 1977 from the Architecture Department at Tamkang University, Taipei, after which he worked as a builder/constructor. In the late 1980s he designed several factories at Hsin Chu Science Park. He won the competition for the Hsin Chu Cultural Center (1992) and Hakka Museum at Kaohsiung (1994). He has been prominent in proposing many reconstruction ideas, such as 'construction solidarity', after the 1999 earthquake, to help people reconstruct not only their physical but also their living space.

Karl-Heinz Klopf was born in Linz, Austria, where he studied at the University for Artistic and Industrial Design. Based in Vienna, the main concern of his artistic practice is constructed environments and the changes of everyday life in relation to today's technological developments. He works in different media such as video, photography, installations and projects in the context of architecture and urbanism.

Peter Lang received his Bachelors in Architecture from Syracuse University, and completed his PhD in Italian history and urbanism at New York University. He is a Fulbright Fellow and registered architect in the US. He has edited two anthologies, *Mortal City* (1995) and *Suburban Discipline* (1997), and recently co-curated and co-edited with William Menking 'Superstudio: Life Without Objects' for the Design Museum in London. He is assistant professor at Texas A&M University's Santa Chiara Program in Italy, where he teaches theory and design studio. He has previously taught at the School of Architecture at NJIT and the Cooper Union. He is a member of the international group Stalker/ON.

Brian McGrath is an architect and co-founder of urban-interface.com, a collaborative group exploring the relationship between multimedia and urban design. His project Manhattan Timeformations (2000) has received many awards from international arts, architecture and science organisations. He teaches at Columbia and New School Universities, New York, and Chulalongkorn University, Bangkok. He was a senior Fulbright scholar in Thailand in 1998/99 and is currently working with an interdisciplinary team of ecologists and sociologists on the Baltimore Ecosytem Study, and co-authoring a book, *Urban Patch Dynamics*.

Yoshiharu Tsukamoto graduated from the Department of Architecture, Faculty of Engineering at Tokyo Institute of Technology, of which he has been associate professor since 1999. In 1992 he established Atelier Bow-wow with Momoyo Kaijima. The office has received the Tokyo Housing Award (2000) and the Yoshioka Prize for Mini-House, and has recently begun exhibiting art works at international art exhibitions in Fukuoka (Japan), Gwangiu (Korea), Shanghai (China) and Venice(Italy), and at the Walker Art Center, US.

Below
Isolated in a pool of still water, and entirely enveloped in bamboo, the bamboo lounge postulates a unique relationship between nature and the mind.

Great 'Bamboo' Wall

Jeremy Melvin describes how designing a house in the vicinity of the Great Wall of China has redirected Kengo Kuma's architectural interests. Inspired by the ancient monument, Kuma has sought to define the house as a means of enclosure using a native material – bamboo – with all its mythical and organic associations.

Top
South elevation: as the bamboo becomes an integral part of the landscape, so it can begin to form its own topography, here revealing the bamboo room at the heart of the house.

Middle
Main level plan: the generous accommodation of over 500 square metres in total floor area provides for the exigencies of bourgeois life, as well as facilities for contemplating nature and culture.

Bottom
North elevation: under a constant datum of the flat roof, the bamboo stalks drop to find the natural level of the ground.

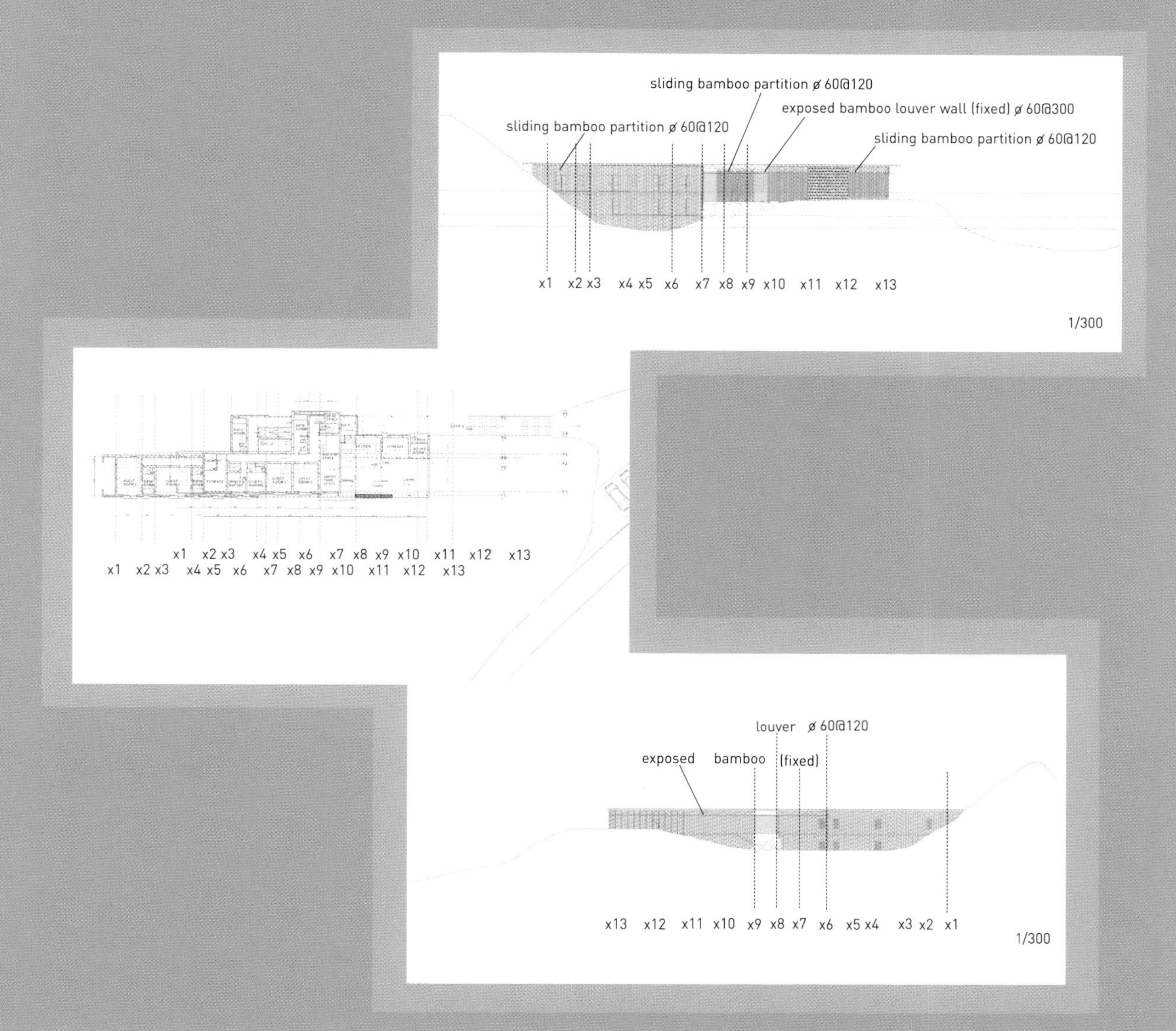

'To me, a house is a floor,' wrote the Japanese architect Kengo Kuma a few years ago about his extraordinary Water/Glass House, 'a sheet of floor floating in nature'.[1] And on that floor, nimbly and delicately, dance the fairies, though fairies can be modern technological devices or traditional fittings. The prospect of designing a house near the Great Wall of China, an hour's drive from Beijing, however, flipped his concept of the house upright as the formal qualities of the wall itself inspired the essence of his vision. 'Our intention,' he says, 'was to apply this nature of the Great Wall to the act of dwelling.' Kuma was one of 12 architects from an emerging Asian generation invited to design houses in the first phase of a speculative housing development on a section near Badaling, the most visited part of the wall.

Developers Pan Shiyi and Zhang Xin aim to create an ecologically aware – if very high value – complex of 11 private houses, and a clubhouse with a cinema, art gallery, restaurant and swimming pool. In a master plan by Hong Kong architect Rocco Yim, Kuma is joined by fellow Japanese architects Shigeru Ban and Nobuaki Furuya, Cui Kai and Yung Ho Chang from China, and Chien Hsueh-Yi, Gary Chang, Kanika R'kul, Kay-Ngee Tan and Seung H-Sang from Taiwan, Hong Kong, Thailand, Singapore and South Korea respectively. Chile's Antonio Ochoa is the only non-Asian, though he has an office in mainland China.

What particularly caught Kuma's eye was the apparent homogeneity of the Great Wall as an object – with its constant cross section it was a megastructure a few millennia before Reyner Banham coined the term – as it contrasts with the varied and dramatic landscapes along its 4,000-mile length. He admired the way it folded itself into the natural topography, and sought to find a way of defining the house through its means of enclosure rather than its floor. In some ways this indicated a new direction for Kuma's architectural interests. When receiving the Spirit of Wood award in Finland in September 2002, he explained that his aim as an architect was to escape from the sense of enclosure that he finds so dominant in 20th-century architecture, defined by steel and concrete.

Top two images
Cross sections

Bottom two images
Long sections.

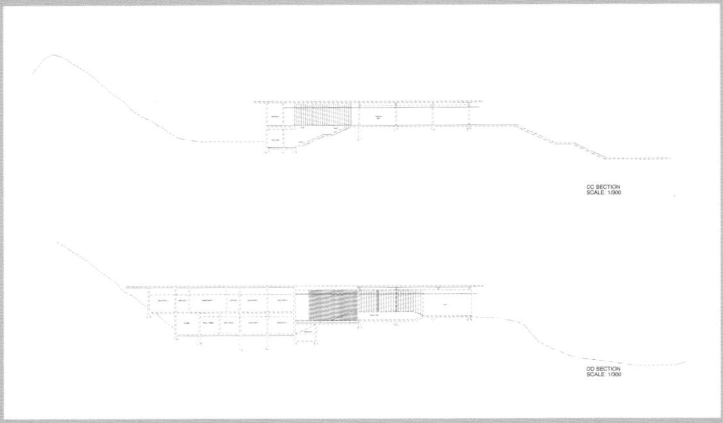

CC SECTION
SCALE: 1/300

DD SECTION
SCALE: 1/300

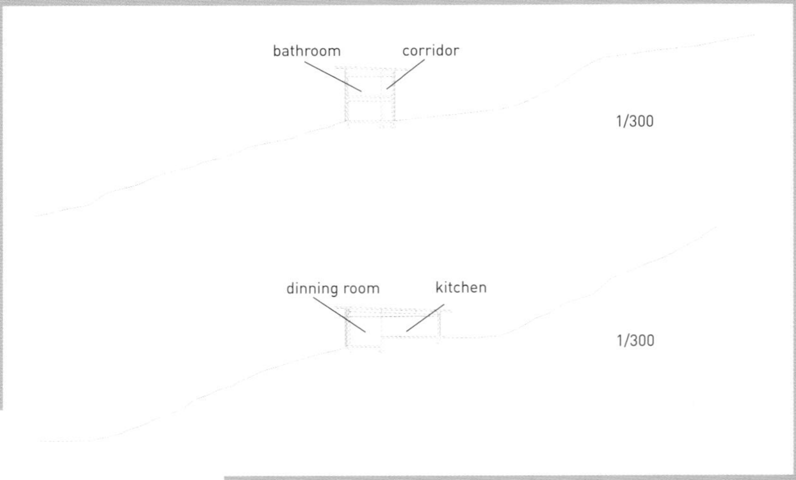

bathroom
corridor
1/300

dinning room
kitchen
1/300

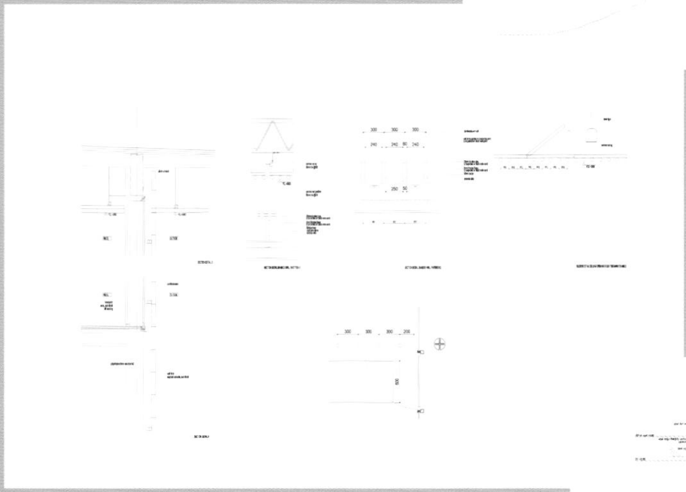

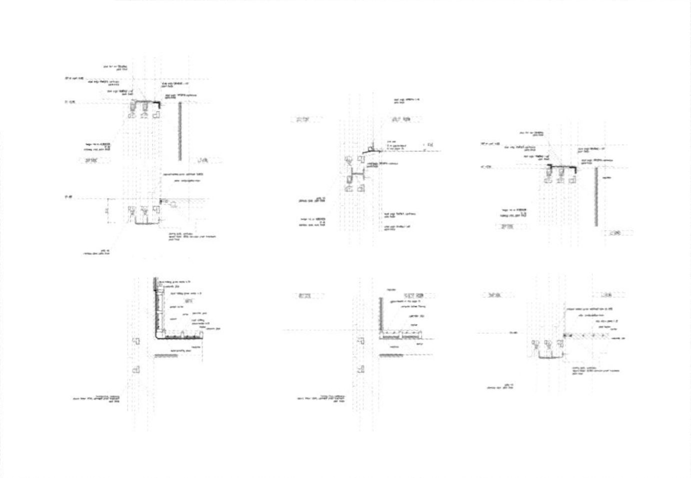

Top
The idea of a central core, which became the bamboo lounge, with planes sliding past each other to define the surrounding spaces, emerged early in the design.

Middle
A sketch of the south elevation begins to explore how the vertical stalks of bamboo might interact with the topography and programme of the house.

Bottom
Early sketches have a passing resemblance to Mies's house in the mountains, of the late 1930s. Even Kuma's realisation of the idea establishes a very different engagement with nature.

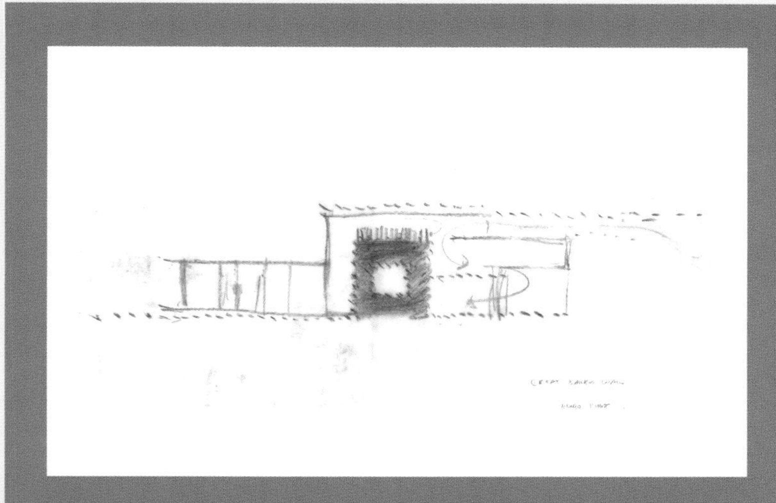

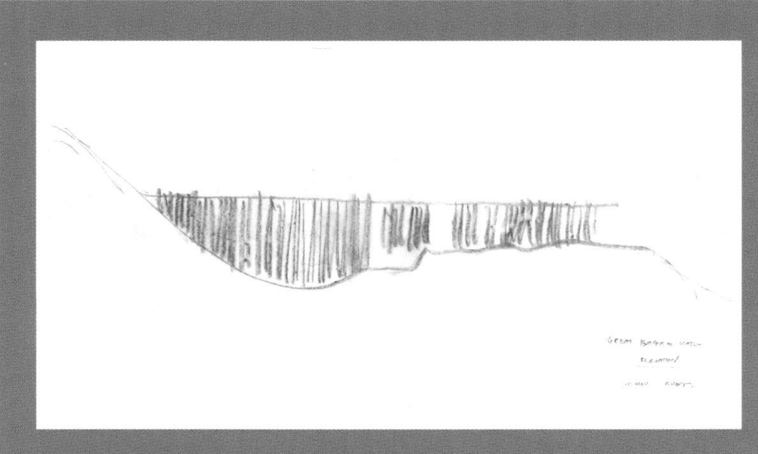

And writing on 'Asian Time' for *Asia Design Forum*, he explained '... to me Asia is chaos, and my objective as an architect is creating chaos'. The whole point of the Great Wall, though, was to separate chaos from order, barbarity from civilisation. In one of those inversions that ruthless application of extreme logic can sometimes generate, Kuma's interpretation of the essence of 'wall' sets itself against the purpose of the Great Wall.

But just as the Great Wall is a sophisticated and subvertible object, so a sense of enclosure can be rendered more ambiguous than a bland means of enclosure. Representing an extreme where fierce pragmatism generates its own mythology, the Great Wall offered the possibility of analogies with fairies dancing on the floor. Not surprisingly Kuma decided to explore them through the notion of 'wall', and in particular through the material he chose to enclose the house – bamboo.

To Kuma, bamboo is a skin rather than just a surface. Both permeable and suggestive of an inner quality, it combines organic and mythic resonances. Its permeability evokes the idea of a skin and to Kuma a skin is not just a membrane around a living body but also defines a place where the soul can reside, and this quality is captured in a Japanese children's tale about the Princess Kakuyahime, the Moon Goddess. Kakuyahime, so the fable runs, was born inside a stalk of bamboo, the peculiar type of skin of which suggested the presence of a soul within. Potentially, each stalk of bamboo can contain a different soul, but for practical purposes Kuma has stiffened them by filling them with steel and concrete, their assembly into a wall generating the overall effect. A bamboo wall can still separate civilisation from barbarity or, more prosaically, inside from outside, but it also permits flows of light and air, a characteristic that fits with bamboo's symbolism of cultural interchange – historically it was imported from Japan to China.

Straddling an undulating site, the house establishes a horizontal datum not with its floor but with its roof: an early sketch shows it hovering in the air, as if the charged ground and delicate bamboo stalks interact to create a momentarily stable equilibrium. It is this datum that distinguishes the house from the Great Wall, the height of which is constant with the result that its top undulates with the ground, while the bamboo, as if hanging, then defines the spatial and lighting conditions that permit the act of dwelling. Approached at an oblique angle up a stepped path, the house looms almost like a temple. However, inside the varied qualities of the bamboo reveal themselves. Seen from an angle the stalks seem continuous, but looked at directly the gaps between them become apparent. At times the striated

Top
Approached via a stepped path, the Great (Bamboo) Wall recalls a classical temple in its visceral connection between nature and artifice.

Middle
The house is a discreet element in a dramatic landscape.

Bottom
Throughout the interior, bamboo and its effects are present in the gently insistent verticality of the screens or the oblique striations of its shadow across the floor and furniture. Every movement is potentially a dance.

light that falls through them anticipates the characteristics of the space. At others it is the views through them that establish the qualities, a switch between abstraction and specificity that reinforces the sense of interchange and echoes the role of the Great Wall as a divider between two very different world-views.

With six bedrooms and space for staff, the house is large but will probably not be a family house. The varying degrees of permeability and definition do not imply the generational or gender relationships that structure families; instead they are more abstract and contemplative. At the heart of the house is a 'bamboo room', isolated in a pool of still water, a retreat where the outside world is transfigured into patterns of light and shade and carefully contrived views to the wilderness beyond. Other rooms are more specific in function though varied in material. The dining room slips from hard-surfaced enclosure to a glazed end, while the sitting room looks from a glazed corner as if into a forest of bamboo.

Such a project will always be strange, but Kuma's design capitalises on the inherent strangeness to create a series of haunting images and impressions. It may not set repeatable patterns for domestic architecture, but it does explore the way a particular material can create varied conditions and use those conditions and effects to resonate with one of humankind's most dramatic artefacts, through them becoming a commentary on broader cultural concerns. ⌂

Note
1 Kisho Kurokawa and Kengo Kuma (eds) *Japanese Avant-Garde: Reality/Projection*, Shokokusha (Tokyo), 2001.

Below
East Modern Art Centre, Beijing, 2001
This art centre and real-estate office are located in an old textile factory where there were plans to cut a new road right through the structure. Removing half of the existing building was the only way to avoid total demolition, so the ragged edge where the water-drill surgery took place has been left as it was, preserving the process of mutilation and making it part of the building's story. Glass channels have been inserted in the concrete structure where the cut was made. On the north side of the renovated building is a garden laid out as a parallel sequence of trees, pavements, water and other textures and volumes, so the indoor space at the southern end can be understood as another layer of the striated landscape.

Yung Ho Chang

In some ways, Yung Ho Chang is much like his native land today – Chinese with American influences, increasingly operating in an international community, and making an impact abroad while absorbing influences for use at home. But instead of pushing Buicks and Texas-sized apartments, he is looking for appropriate indigenous solutions to uniquely Chinese problems. **Jayne Merkel** explains how he got into this unusual position and how he is using his experience to help create a new kind of architecture at home.

Educated first in China and then in the US, Yung Ho Chang spent the first 10 years of his career teaching in America. He then returned to Beijing and started the firm Atelier Feichang Jianzhu, with his wife Ljia Lu, though he continued to commute to the US for three more years. 'In 1996 I realised that I couldn't do both – spending so much time away from the practice where my mind was most of the time,' he said, 'so I quit the teaching job in the US.' But a few years later came an offer he couldn't refuse – to start a new graduate programme at Peking University. (Yes, Peking. 'Three things in Beijing are still called Peking,' Chang explains, 'the opera, the duck and the university, because they are so old. You never say "Beijing Opera"; you say "Peking Opera", "Peking duck" and "Peking University".')

So he is now teaching and practising again, and in autumn 2002 he took to the air once more to hold the Kenzo Tange Chair at Harvard. He's also in Europe a lot, participating in various international exhibitions.

All these crosscurrents, of course, put Chang in a unique position to help develop an authentic contemporary Chinese architecture which, along with a related urbanism, is his main concern. His fresh approach to this is partly the result of a serendipitous early encounter at Ball State University in Indiana with South African teacher Rodney Place, who had studied with Peter Cook at the Architectural Association in London.

'Rodney Place taught in a very Zen-like manner. He wouldn't ever offer any answers. He would just raise all sorts of questions. He tortured us! If you gave him an answer, he wouldn't say anything, and he would make this most painful face. It could be really, really bad!' During those years, Chang developed an interest in art, especially Marcel Duchamp, New Wave French films and new novels – none of which had been included in his Chinese education.

The first postmodern attempts in China to create a new indigenous architecture were the little pagoda-like

Below

Xishu Book Store, Beijing, 1996

Atelier Feichang Jianzhu's first completed project was a book store in a 1957 building that had been designed for vehicular traffic and used for bicycles as well. To recall its history and make it easy for the store owners to reorganise the space when they needed to, the architects placed the book shelves on bicycle wheels, which have solid rubber tyres to hold the weight of the books. 'Bookbikes' stand guard at the entrance, making books immediately available while setting the tone for the theme of the space. A new mezzanine is currently being added.

roofs on tall buildings in Beijing. 'Those Chinese "hats" were pushed by one particular mayor who fell a few years ago, in a rather disgraceful way. But he had this great concern with architectural identity in the city. He wasn't an architect, though, so he couldn't come up with a better idea than that,' Chang explained, adding that though they were not the right solution, 'now we have this international style of corporate architecture. Which way is better? I don't know!.'

'When I first went back, over 10 years ago, people would hire Hong Kong architects, although they couldn't really do better work than the locals could. That phase is now long gone,' he said. Then came Western corporate firms, such as SOM and KPF (which was especially popular a few years ago). Now GMP from Frankfurt, and RTKL from Baltimore, are very active, along with the big Chinese firms that have an increasing share of the business. The biggest are the Beijing Institute of Architectural Design Research, an outgrowth of the Beijing Municipal Architectural Office (where Chang's father worked as an architect all his life) and the Modern Group in Shanghai. Since Rem Koolhaas won the China Centre Television Headquarters he has received more attention, along with architects like Tadeo Ando (who came to China to lecture and was treated like a pop star), Kazuyo Sejima, MVRDV and other architects who are published in Western magazines, which are very popular in China today.

However, Chang feels that the most promising work is being done by small Asian firms, such as those who designed low-cost houses for the Commune by the Great Wall – Shigeru Ban, Gary Chang, Chien Hsueh-Yi, Nobuaki Furuya, Cui Kai, Kengo Kuma, Kay Ngee Tan, Antonio Ochoa, Kanika R'kul, Rocco Yim and Seung H-Sang (the Korean architect responsible for the clubhouse). Yung Ho Chang designed one of the houses.

Chang's Split House for the Commune, of 2002, is divided in the middle to let in the landscape. Its traditional Chinese courtyard is enclosed by the nearby mountains on one side and the walls of the house on the other, blurring the line between the natural and the man-made. The structural frame is made of laminated wood. The house has rammed-earth walls, an ancient technique that provides good insulation with minimal environmental impact. And it could be a prototype because the angle between the halves can be adjusted to accommodate various hilly sites.

A natural response to climate is part of Chang's search for an appropriate indigenous architecture, since the advent of air conditioning in the 1980s erased the differences between buildings in different regions. Atelier Feichang Jianzhu's Shipai Town Hall has a framing colonnade on the south side that provides both an appropriate image for a government building and sun shading in the hot and muggy Pearl River Delta.

Chang's concern for suitable siting led to his interest in urbanism. On moving back to Beijing he 'began to realise that urbanisation is impacting people's lives more than individual buildings'. He wondered: 'Can we

Below

Shipai Town Hall, Dongguan, 2002

The administrative centre of one the 33 townships of Dongguan city in the Pearl River Delta responds to hot, humid local weather conditions to achieve a regional architecture of a sort that disappeared with the introduction of air conditioning in the 1980s. On the south side, a framing colonnade creates an image of government while serving as a sun-shading device. The building has also been sliced east to west into three thin layers to provide natural ventilation. Horizontal louvres on top of the complex define public spaces between the layers and reduce heat gain on the roof.

Below
Villa Shan Yu Jian (Mountain Dialogue Space), Beijing, 1998
In order to interact with the surrounding landscape as much as possible without disrupting the existing terraced farmland, the house follows the slope of the hill with views all around. A large roof supported on a steel frame floats over the site, conceptually reconstructing the hillside. Beneath the roof, a continuous living space is divided into mini buildings by thick box-like walls, while large areas of glass on all sides invite the landscape inside, so the terraced farmland is rebuilt in an architectural way instead of obliterated as landscape often is in China. Three attic guest-rooms poke through the roof revealing the spatial structure of the interior and presenting themselves as detached houses on the slope.

have a contemporary Chinese architecture without a definition of what a contemporary Chinese city is? Besides,' he notes, 'in present-day China architects actually have opportunities to design and build cities.'

It is difficult not to think about urbanism in Beijing as it is enormous, fast growing, congested and car-dependent. It has 13 million people but this is expected to reach 16 million by the 2008 Olympics.

Chang realised just how spread out the city is whilst in Rome: 'I looked at a map to see where the Coliseum was. From the urban scale I'm used to, I imagined it would take an hour to walk, and I was there in 20 minutes or less. Then when Richard Ingersoll came to Beijing, he thought he would be able to walk from the Forbidden City to the Temple of Heaven, also, in about an hour. He walked for about five hours. If you look at the map of Beijing, they do seem very close. But the city is tremendous. When I was little, I lived on the east side of the city and never had any need to go to the west side, ever. Now people need to move around a lot, and it's not walkable. That's why so many people are getting cars. (Shanghai, on the other hand, is a very walkable city.)'

Though there is a subway system in Beijing it has only two lines, in the centre. A plan to extend the system does exist, but this 'is sponsored by the government, and the government doesn't have the money to push it very fast. Meanwhile, the roads are built by industry, with no money from the state, so they are growing really fast,' says Chang. 'Two or three years ago there was a projection of 1.2 million cars by the year 2010, and then last year, two years after that estimate was made, there were 1.7 million cars. And they tend to be big American ones. Buicks are very popular. The roads are really, really jammed.'

Relying on American models also creates problems in housing. Though the new housing towers are 22 to 30 storeys high, until recently the units were fairly large (100 to 120 square metres) despite the fact that efficient smaller ones, like those in Japan, would make more sense. The blocks in Beijing are large and the streets are wide, though Chang's studies show that more smaller streets, like those in New York, would move traffic better. His students are currently working on the scale of the city: 'In Beijing, one of my students is constructing a kind of urban space by taking panoramic photographs of various roads in the city. He has taken probably up to 30 different roads. At Harvard that's difficult to do, so we're doing an exercise of raising the density of the city from the original floor-area ratio of 0:3, all the way up to 5.'

Chang's students at Peking University are also working on materials research and construction technology – two of his other concerns that are important for a new Chinese architecture. Students are given a budget and have to build their projects. A model home Chang designed in Beijing had a water courtyard made with bamboo, and though this didn't turn out as planned he is now trying to use bamboo for a curtain wall.

The trick will be to employ elements and materials that have been used in the past in new ways, as in the rammed-earth wall. As the city grows exponentially, further controls and new forms will be called for. However, Western-style zoning will not be the answer: 'The Chinese notion of zoning is very different. Basically it's an introverted neighbourhood, with some kind of segregation.' In the past the Mandarins lived in one area, the Chinese in another, the aristocrats in their own quarter, and the common people in theirs. Instead of neighbourhood stores, like those in Shanghai and European or American cities, in Beijing 'it was something totally unique. You lived in an alleyway, called a "*hu-tong*". For everyday shopping you didn't have to go anywhere. All kinds of vendors would come to your door to sell you everything from fresh fruit to a haircut, to fixing your broken chinaware. For everyday things you could just stay in your own house, waiting for all the services.'

Today there are regular stores, even chain stores, with very long store-fronts so it is not possible to walk down a block the way you can in Hong Kong or New York, and pass a dozen shops. It is necessary to drive from one to another, and there is a terrible parking problem. The only things sold door-to-door are pirated CDs and architecture books.

Below

Southwest China Bio-Tech Pilot Base, Chongqing, 2001

This single building, on the south bank of the Yangtze River, is composed of several separate but connected parts to accommodate a mixed programme of research laboratories, production laboratories, offices and hotel rooms. Two parallel concrete-block facades unify the various quarters while a series of penetrations accentuates their independence. In order to comply with a local code, the building had to be set back from the sloping river-bank, but a number of passageways composed of flights of stairs tie it to the landscape, connect the street on one side with the river on the other, and create courtyards on top of offices.

Below

Split House, Yanqing, Beijing, for the Commune by the Great Wall, 2002

Located in the mountains of northern Beijing, the house is divided down the middle to bring the landscape into what would otherwise be a traditional Chinese courtyard, conceptually forming an interior wall. Since it is in an area being returned to nature, the structural frame is made of laminated wood and the walls are made of well-insulating, compressed, rammed earth, created by using the same kind of formwork as that used for concrete.

Below
Peking University International Conference Centre, Qingdao, 2001
The steeply sloping ocean-side site, where the elevation drops 20 metres from the access road to the water, inspired an architecture here that offers an experience of descending to the sea. The building form provides a linear sequence of interior and exterior platforms and staircases. Five existing villas were remodelled for the hotel component of the centre, their roofs made accessible to constitute other levels of topographical formation.

Yung Ho Chang Resumé

1956	Born in Beijing, China
1978–81	Nanjing Institute of Technology
1984	BS Environmental Design, Ball State University, Muncie, Indiana
1984	MArch, University of California, Berkeley
1986	First place, Shinkenchiku Residential Design Competition, Japan
1992	Winner, Steedman Traveling Fellowship, Washington University, St Louis, Missouri
	Young Architects Forum, Architectural League of New York
1993	Established Atelier Feichang Jianzhu in Beijing with Lija Lu
1996	Xishu Book Store interior, Beijing
	Progressive Architecture magazine awards citation
1996–98	Professor, Rice University, Houston, Texas
1997	Cummins Engine Company Asia Office, Beijing
1998	Morningside Centre for Mathematics, Chinese Academy of Sciences, Beijing
	Hillside Housing, Shenzhen
	Villa Shan Yu Jian (Mountain Dialogue Space), Beijing
1999	'Street Theater', solo exhibition, Apex Gallery, New York
	Crystal Imaging Office, Beijing
2000	Head and Professor, Graduate Centre for Architecture, Peking University
	Bamboo Screen Door installation, Venice Biennale for Architecture
	New Shanghai House installation, Shanghai
	2000 UNESCO Prize for the Promotion of the Arts
2001	Southwest China Bio-Tech Pilot Base, Chongqing
	Peking University International Conference Centre, Qingdao
	East Modern Art Centre, Beijing
2002	Shipai Town Hall, Dongguan
	Split House, Yanqing, Beijing, for the Commune by the Great Wall
	Japanese Pavilion installation and Split House at the Commune by the Great Wall, Venice Architectural Biennale
	Kenzo Tange Chair and 'Six Crates of Architecture' solo exhibition, Harvard Graduate School of Design
2003	*Yung Ho Chang/Atelier Feichang Jianzhu: A Chinese Practice*, monograph to be published by Map Books, Hong Kong
	'Camera, Paris', an exhibition installation in collaboration with video artists Wang Jianwei and Yang Fudong, Museum of Modern Art, Paris
	Venice (Art) Biennale 4

Below
Boston Harbor Lights Pavilion
Architect/engineer: FTL
Detail of membrane plate showing the resolution of complex performance and aesthetic requirements in the mechanical design of architectural components, tasks that can be aided greatly by development of collaborative design tools.

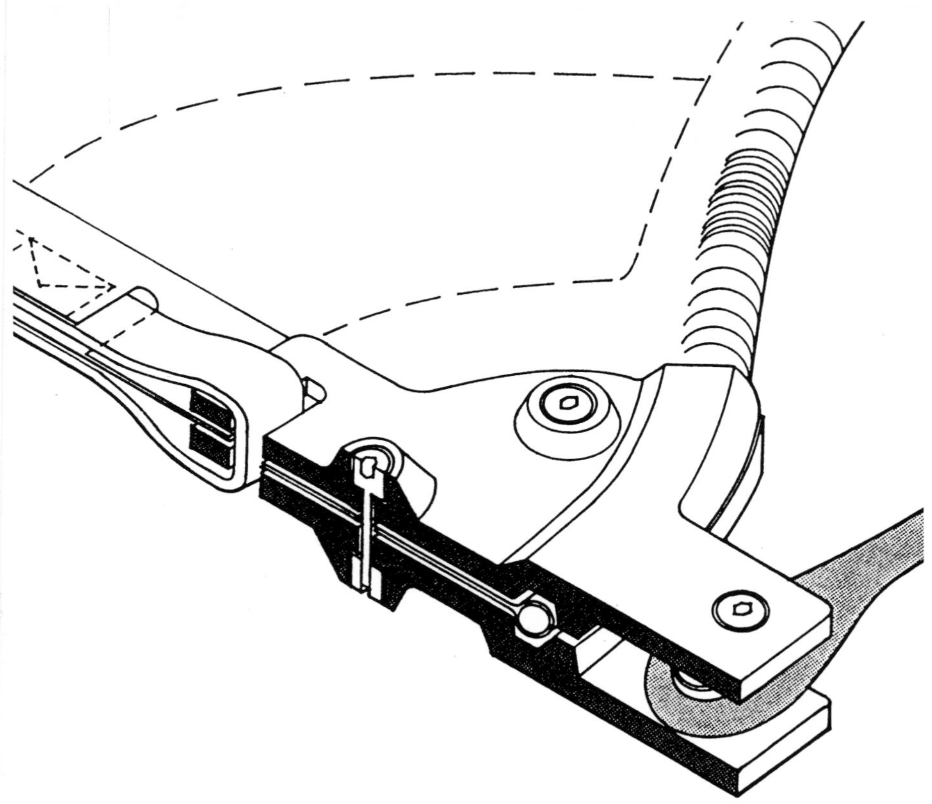

Bridging the Gap with Collaborative Design Programs for CAD/CAM

Successfully bringing together the capabilities that CAD/CAM confers, such as those described in the previous four articles in the 'Blurring the Lines' series, requires that we leverage the communicative advantages of computers in order to enable both the effective integration of various specialists' inputs and the effective use of information in the successive stages from the conception of a project to its execution. Much of the software currently available for analysis and design already enables this to some extent, and the generative design tools on the horizon may enable even greater integration of 'work flow'. However, as **André Chaszar** argues in the following article, better collaborative design programs are needed to bridge the gap between the capabilities of present digital tools and the next generation of architectural design.

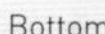

Top
Astler-Parker Residence
Architect: Atelier Wylde-Oubrerie Engineer: O-Design
System model of wave-form roof showing development of alternative rulings, skinning for visual evaluation and finally unfolding for analysis of cladding fabrication.

Bottom
Vari-beam
Engineer: O-Design
The digital model of a variable-section I-beam shows an envelope of depths required for structural performance, as well as the twisting deformation required when the element is placed in the context of the wave-form roof. A reduced level of detail is preferred for visualisation when checking whether the degree of twist falls within the specified limits.

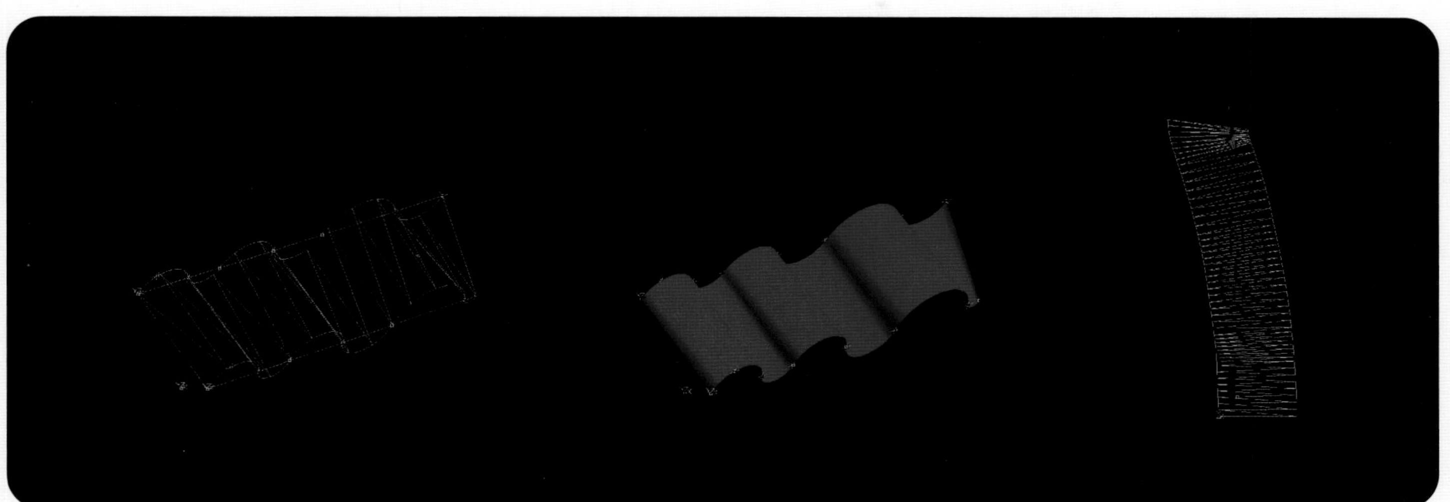

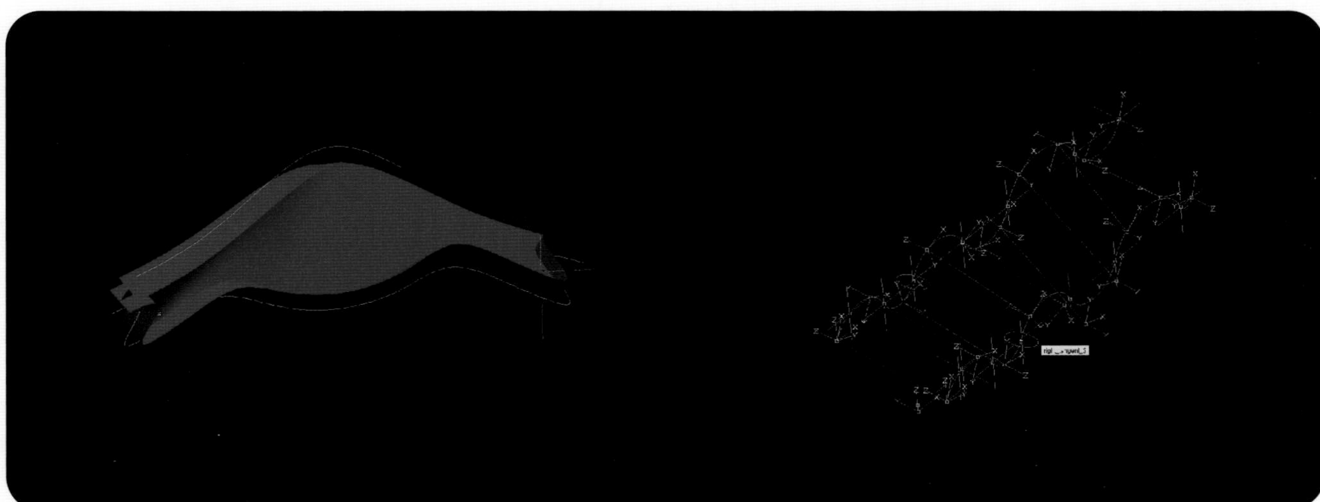

Collaborative design processes are generally recognised as those in which the participants are of various disciplines (design, construction or otherwise) and engage in closely linked, parallel development of the aspects of the project for which they are themselves responsible. This kind of process is also generally recognised as enabling execution of projects with much greater than average complexity and refinement. Perhaps the most important ingredient of a collaboration such as this is an attitudinal one: willingness to engage the views of others on the project team and to work out the differences that are sure to arise (whether from personal approaches or inevitably conflicting project requirements), seeing these tensions as potentially positive events that can test ideas in the arena of reality and thus strengthen them. Without such willingness, collaboration can hardly make any headway, but once this foundation is in place the collaborators need some tools to assist them.

Collaborative tools in the present sense are those that offer the following:

- rapid feedback on the consequences of design, procurement or installation decisions, whether to a single user, a single-discipline group, or to a multidisciplinary group;
- readily interpretable results, achieved, for example, through carefully selected classes of information and good graphical and alphanumeric display of these;
- facilitatation of substantive real-time design exploration and discussion of results among relevant parties, for example by incorporating clearly legible methods of display and interactive mark-up capabilities for face-to-face collaboration, and additionally by quickly transmitting the necessary information within the available bandwidth

Below, left to right
Wave-form roof model
Engineers: O-Design and Bentley Microsystems
The sequence of different states of the roof shape shows how joists framing it would vary in their degree of twist consistent with the curve slopes and the joining rule stipulated, as well as vary in number due to the changing lengths of the supporting arc-ed beams in accordance with the specified spacing parameters.

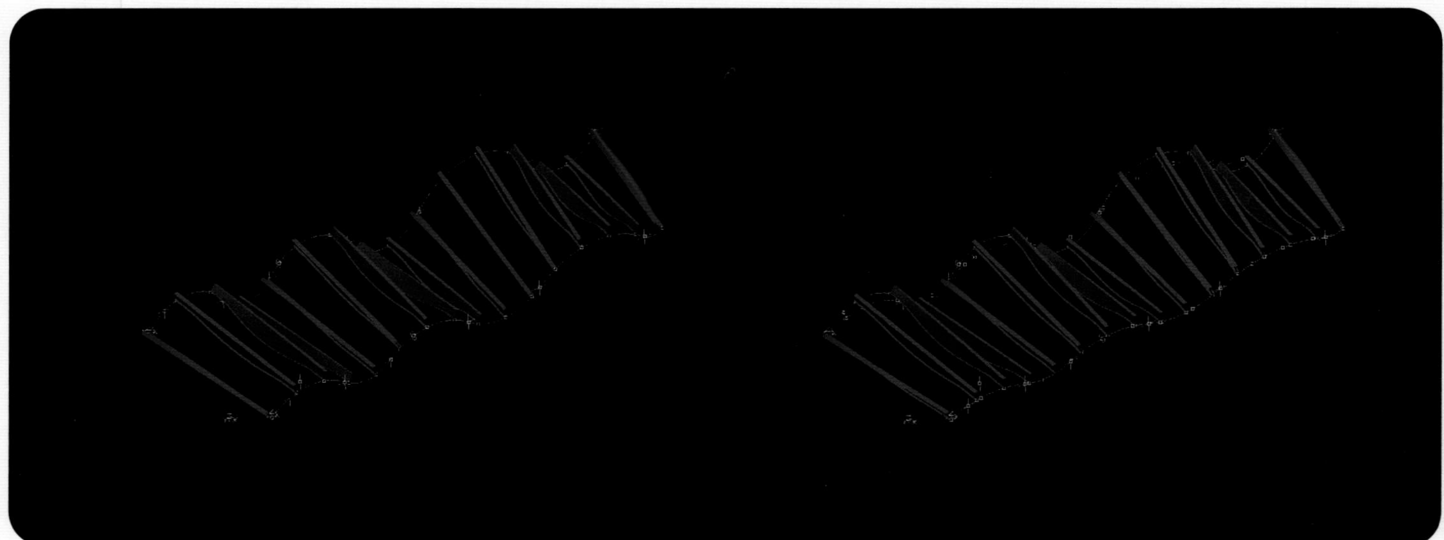

when collaboration occurs remotely. (This may be seen as mainly a hardware issue, but it actually also depends to an enormous extent on user–computer interface design.)

The need for reliability of results of CAD (which here includes CAE (computer-aided engineering) programs), goes without saying, though it must be noted that the other aims of such collaborative tools may preclude the production of highly detailed analyses, for example, and that their use may therefore be restricted to the conceptual/schematic design and 'design development' phases.

Existing collaborative capabilities are found in such high-end software as CATIA and CADS5, which encompass a wide range of sophisticated modelling and analysis tools within a single package, though these require extensive training and are quite expensive, making them generally unsuitable for adoption by the construction industry. Other, industry-specific software such as Shipbuilder has extensive and varied capabilities too – from design through preparation of bills of materials and shop drawings – and is less oriented towards 'power users', which may with some ingenuity make it applicable to buildings.

More limited integration of work flow is achieved with proprietary speciality packages such as Tensyl (which offers vertical integration from design visualisation and 'form finding' through structural analysis to fabrication information for fabric-and-cable structures) and a variety of steel detailers' programs, perhaps the most widely adopted of which – X-Steel – offers visualisation and analysis capabilities as well as producing connection details and bills of materials for steel-framed structures (but not concrete, wood or any other structural materials, or for architectural assemblies in general).

Beyond these, the specialisation of most architecture, engineering and construction (AEC) industry-oriented CAD drafting and modelling, animation, engineering analysis and fabricator support software makes them not particularly well suited to collaborative design or design-and-fabrication processes, rather leading only to potential gains in speed and/or accuracy of work in a conventional 'throw-it-over-the-fence' variety of teamwork. Instead, their successful use in such integrated design environments relies on varying degrees of file input/output compatibility and on the skills of their users in producing results that are readily digestible by other members of the project team. In some instances these are jury rigged, as with engineers' [Arup] use of animated particles in a ray-tracing algorithm in a CAD package to simulate acoustical phenomena for rapid comprehension by the Greater London Authority project's architects [Foster Partners]. (See the first article in the 'Blurring the Lines' series: *AD*, 'Off the Radar', vol 73, Jan/Feb 2003.)

In the case of metal castings, as described by Tim Eliassen, the fabrication and engineering capabilities were integrated under one roof (perhaps even in a single person). If this were not the case, the communication circle would have to be expanded at least to include a separate engineer performing stress analysis on the metal part, and even perhaps another contractor to comment upon the installation considerations, while both the fabricator and installer would be needed to evaluate the economic impacts of the design. At certain times in the evolution of the design, it would be desirable for all of these parties

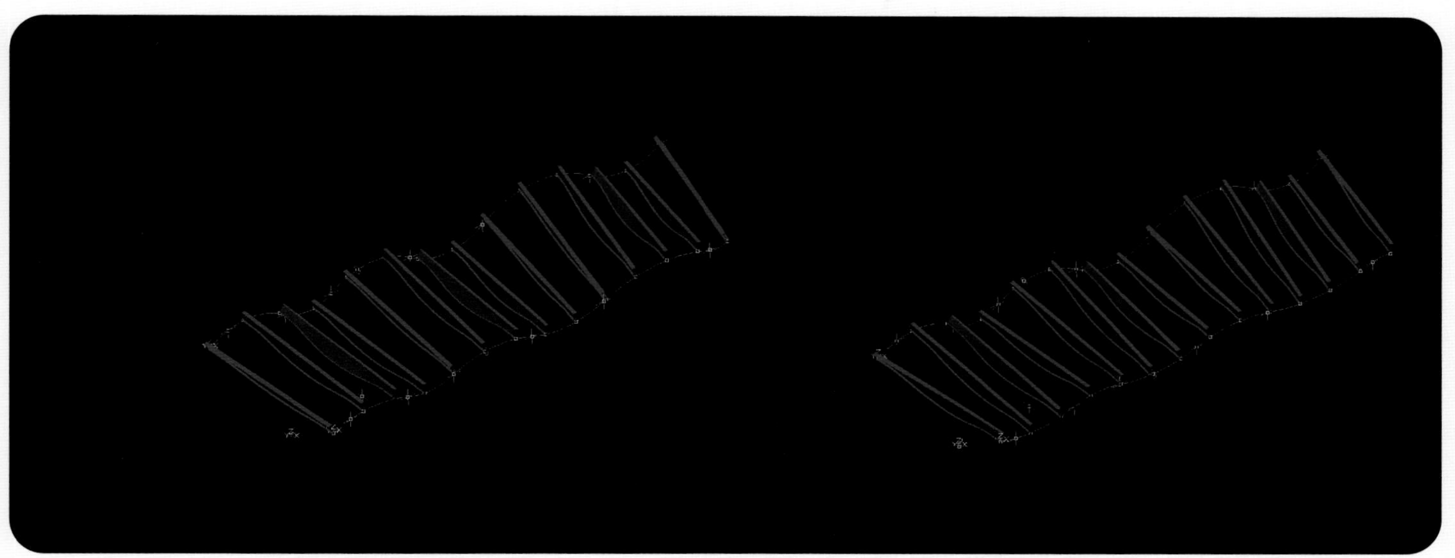

to be looking at the same information (digital model and alphanumeric data) simultaneously, and moreover to be subsequently watching and commenting on the results of the various design modifications being made even as they happened. If, as in the case of cost estimating, some sort of off-line analysis must be made, this too must take place in 'real time' to maintain the momentum of the collaboration. Again, assuming the willingness of the parties, the challenges are: first, to program tools able to do this; second, to design and implement the interfaces that allow the resulting information to be displayed, digested and acted on; and third, to make these tools available and accessible to architects, engineers and builders who are not necessarily programmers as well.

Programmers have a role, of course, in the initial development and subsequent refinement of the tools by the software companies who produce them or, in the case of certain large enough design firms, in producing them in-house. Moreover, programmers will have a continuing involvement at the end-users' end as the available tools need to be customised from time to time, project to project, or as their firms' work flows evolve. This will continue to be the case for the forseeable future unless enormous advances are soon made in the development of visual programming tools. Even then it seems inevitable that the education or on-the-job training of designers and builders will have to include a greater measure of programming than at present in order for the full potential of collaborative (and even non-collaborative) CAD/CAM tools to be realised. In the meantime, architects, engineers and contractors must be vocal regarding the capabilities they wish the software to possess.

A few examples serve to illustrate the opportunities and problems posed by collaborative CAD or CAD/CAM tools:

1 a wave-form roof, dealing with the design of a complex system or sub-system;
2 a variable-section beam, addressing the design and fabrication of a complex, customised component;
3 a 'membrane plate' that is a specialised building component, the design of which might possibly be 'automated' with generative tools; and
4 the selection and/or evaluation of window area in relation to floor area, illustrative of a class of rule-of-thumb or simplified methods also applicable to preliminary HVAC, acoustical and structural design tasks, among others.

The wave-form roof problem stems from a situation fairly common in contemporary architectural design, where the architect seeks to produce some sort of complexly curved surface. Although many available surface- and solid-type CAD, animation or other programs allow the designer to digitally model forms and subsequently modify the digital model until a satisfactory shape is achieved (possibly even employing physical models to be initially scanned and then digitised, or using rapid prototyping to produce physical solid or templated models for direct visual and tactile evaluation), the more significant problem is that of establishing that the shape is actually constructible at full scale and can meet certain budgetary and schedule requirements. In order to effect this type of evaluation, the conventional (and still prevalent) process would be an 'over-the-fence' exercise, in which the the architect's drawings of the form – or in a slightly more advanced scenario, the actual digital data from the architect's model – are

Below left
Ladies Pavilion
Architect: Peter Dew and Associates Engineer: Buro Happold
The highlighted area indicates the typical location of a 'membrane plate' in a fabric-and-cable tensile structure, where it resolves the forces and geometries of the system's conjoining elements. Fabric, cables and tie rods of varying sizes and arrangements at various points on the structure require subtle or extreme variations in the features of the plates.

Below right
AT&T Olympic Pavilion
Architect/engineer: FTL
Detail of membrane plate showing how conforming to performance requirements may still result in a highly stylised object, indicating the range of possibilities that the parametrically or associatively manipulated digital model may need to encompass.

transmitted to engineers and/or contractors for their subsequent analysis. Naturally, accuracy and comprehension of the drawings as well as file compatibility issues are hurdles to be overcome, and once overcome they will resurface again every time the design is passed from one party of the project team to another.

A further serious disadvantage of this process is that the evaulations of the form by the various parties occur mainly in different places and at different times from one another. Thus the continuity and momentum that characterise the most effective collaborative design processes are lost except on rare occasions. Decisions taken by one party are made and communicated with some delay, by which time the thinking of many or most of the other parties will have evolved to the point that the decisions are no longer entirely relevant or valid. (Not all of the work can or should occur 'communally', but the vast majority of projects could benefit from substantially more closely interactive work than they tend to have at present.)

A more effective working paradigm is enabled when the tools (digital or otherwise) used for description and analysis of the design by architects, engineers, contractors and building owners are the same, or more nearly the same. Thus in the wave-form roof design a digital model is built from geometric primitives (lines, arcs, etc) that can be manipulated parametrically as well as by associative geometric operations. (These are user-defined interrelationships among elements that result in reconfigurations more complex than the typical scaling, stretching, copying, rotating and so on, or even the more sophisticated mappings and other distortions found in animation software, for example.) These primitives, or elements, are selected and arranged collaboratively in such a way that they at once describe roughly the characteristics of the shape envisioned by the architect, as well as suggesting a plausible system of construction (as more typically entrusted to the engineer and contractor). This model can be established cooperatively on a fairly common CAD platform (in this case Microstation V8), which may well be part of the normal work flows of the various parties.

Specifically, this model constructed for design development of a residential-scale roof (see page 114) comprises two sinuous lines (beams) constructed from arcs, and a series of crossing lines (joists) that are straight. The arcs are chosen because the beams are provisionally envisioned to be fabricated from steel pipes, and constant-radius bending equipment is fairly common among steel fabricators, whereas specialists would be needed to fabricate such continuously varying curves as result from splines. The arcs are constrained to meet at tangent points in order to offer the simplest splicing details. They are initially further constrained so that their tangent points lie in a straight line and so that they lie in vertical planes. However, note that the two strings of arcs do not necessarily lie in planes parallel to each other, and that the locations and magnitudes of the strings' peaks and valleys, as well as their actual and projected lengths, can be varied independently of each other. These constraints can

Below
The digital model of a membrane plate allows automatic generation of features derived from the context of the element, as well as designer-overrides and freedom of design for other, nondetermined features.

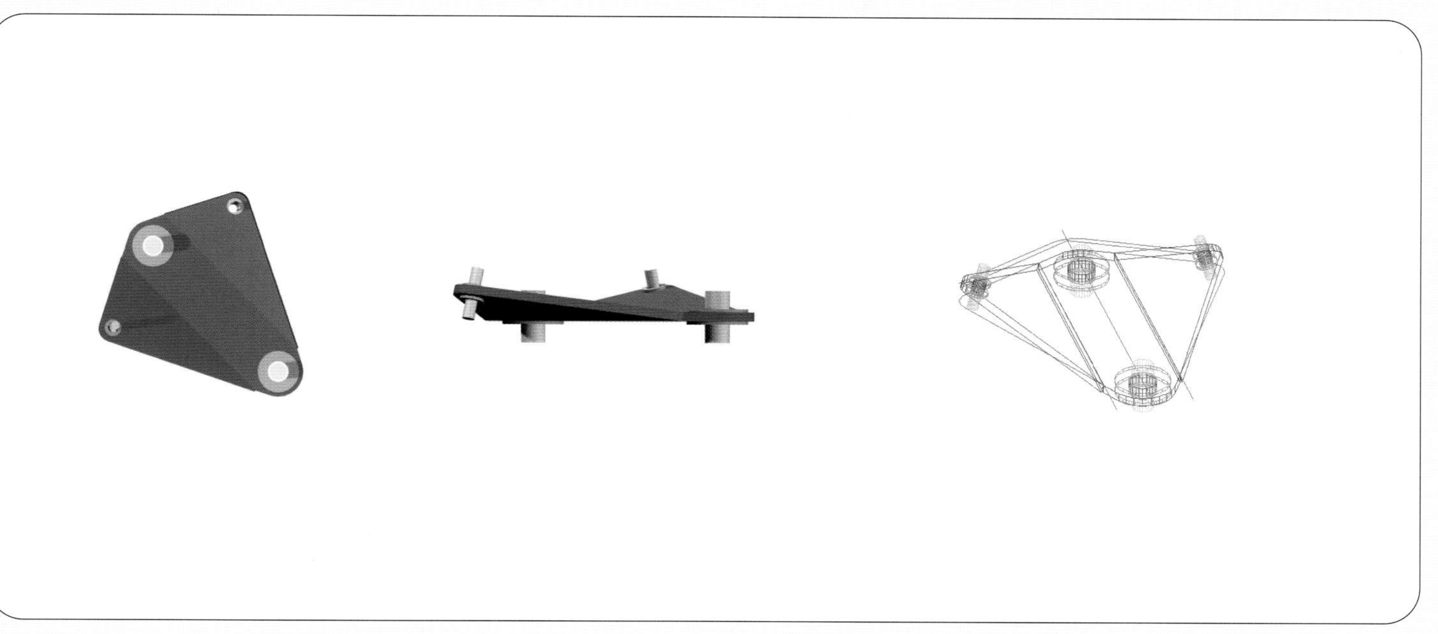

be changed as the design evolves, requiring only some judgement from the designer(s) regarding how much freedom is useful at a particular moment.

Once established, this malleable digital model can be updated in a variety of ways as design options are explored and the design evolves. (For example, the maximum spacing between joists might be parametrically adjusted in response to the choice of decking material.) Designers using such tools need analytical feedback, for example through graphics displaying the joists' slope, degree of twist or any of a number of other important features. Of course, at some stage in the process the design may evolve in a direction different enough that the initial (though by now significantly modified) model is no longer appropriate and a new model must be built that incorporates some or none of the other's elements. Clearly no system is universal. This realisation also underscores the importance of ensuring that the modelling software is sufficiently approachable to allow construction of a new model without undue effort, and moreover without risking the bottlenecks resulting when only specially trained programmers/operators can build new models.

The three other examples briefly illustrate some additional points. The model of a variable-section beam is again created from geometric primitives, then manipulated parametrically through direct input and spreadsheet-calculated values as well as geometrically through mouse operations on screen. For a given uniform load and a given span – possibly derived from a system-level model such as the wave-form roof – empirically determined values for allowable stresses and elasticity are used to calculate and plot the depth envelopes required for shear, moment and deflection (assuming an 'I' section with a given web thickness and flanges of specified, constant width and thickness). The resulting envelope can be used during schematic design and design development for immediate feedback regarding the minimum joist or beam depth required as span lengths and spacings change through the architects' manipulation of the system model. In fact, if the envelope results are taken literally, the web and flange profiles can be used as templates for manual cutting or through file conversions for direct CNC cutting of sheet material and fabrication of a variable-section beam. This also illustrates the power of relatively simple materials and cutting equipment to produce complex forms in a digital environment.

Another mechanical design problem involving more detailing and a greater degree of variability is posed by the membrane plates used to terminate and join cables, fabric and other components at the node points of tensile structures. Many of the required characteristics of the plate can be derived relatively linearly from data such as material strength, allowable stresses and applied forces. Cable and clevis sizes derived from these (or overridden by the designers) lead to pin sizes, which lead to hole sizes and edge distances. The tangent angles of incoming cables (imported from a structural analysis package), clearances between pin holes and local thickening with bosses to accommodate large bearing forces

Below
The 3-D model of a simple room relating the area of glazing on its wall to the floor area demonstrates the cognitive complexity of even some seemingly simple design tasks. Even in such a highly constrained 'problem space', the number of possible, arguably acceptable solutions is significant, and the design tools that seek to aid in solving them must avoid directing the designer to a particular one.

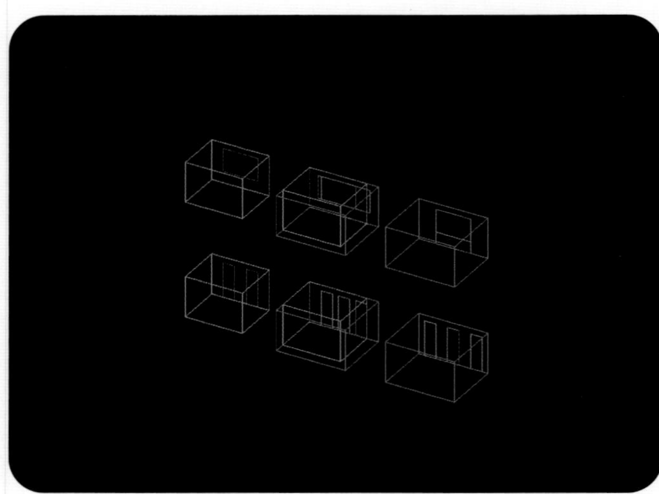

lead to general layout and spacing of the terminations. Resolving the 3-D geometry deftly allows fabrication of the complex plate from a flat sheet simply folded one or more times. Plate-cutting paths can be generated for CNC equipment, and if necessary, welds located by the designers can also be sized using the strength and force parameters.

Through all this the opportunity exists to greatly speed up and simplify the largely repetitive task of designing similar elements with some variations that may occur dozens or even hundreds of times in a single project, one of the most often proclaimed advantages of CAM. The challenge here is to do this in a way that is not only reliable but also affords the flexibility required by unusual situations and creative designers. Again, since no 'master plate model' can realistically be expected to cover all possible design requirements, the modelling tool must be reprogrammable, preferably without resorting to special programming skills and the bottlenecks that can result thereby.

Lastly, the relatively simply stated design problem of relating the floor area and volume of a room to the quantity and arrangement of glazing in its walls illuminates the considerable sophistication of logical control needed when the design task is not linear and where more than one acceptable solution is clearly available. In laying out a simple, rectangular space with flat floor and ceiling, and for argument's sake windows on only one of the four walls, building code requirements or other rules of thumb for daylighting may dictate a certain minimum area of glazing. (Note that energy conservation requirements may, on the other hand, dictate a maximum area of glazing, and these requirements may not necessarily be compatible.)

A model is constructed allowing graphical and/or parametric modification of the plan size and shape of the room, as well as the height of its ceiling. A single rectangular area is modelled on one wall, representing a window.

The most straightforward approach might suggest that varying the plan size of the room should result in a proportional change in window area, while maintaining that window's aspect ratio. But of course the facade design may give preference to a scheme that varies only the width, not height, or height but not width, of the window. In this latter case, should the sill height remain constant, or the head height, or does the designer prefer some other relationship that does not simply centre the window in the wall? Or if standard window sizes are to be used, then it is not the dimensions of a single window that are to be varied but the quantity of discrete windows of fixed area, and what then is the tolerance for glazing area above or below the requirement? At this point we haven't even begun to consider the effects on light of wall thickness, or distance of the window edges from floor, ceiling and sidewalls – though in all fairness we may decide that these considerations are not relevant at this particular design stage.

It is thus apparent that even some fairly elementary design tasks reveal themselves to be surprisingly complex when we attempt to explicitly delineate the various decisions a designer may make almost subconsciously. To some extent this is a challenge not only for software development but for cognitive science to help us here. If successful, however, these efforts will certainly pay off in the speed, accuracy, inventiveness and thoroughness with which we design and construct buildings. Again, the argument is not that collaborative tools as understood here are not already available to some extent, but that their capabilities are as yet too narrow and their usefulness will remain limited if access to them is restricted to only a few designers due, for example, to high cost or difficulty of operation requiring extensive training or special nondesign skills.

Furthermore, we should recognise that even with the best skills and intentions, the contractual arrangements prevalent in much of the world mediate against full collaboration, instead encouraging designers and builders to keep in good repair and build ever higher the fences over which they throw the information they have generated in a conventional project approach. ⌂

In the next article in the 'Blurring the Lines' series', Jim Glymph of Gehry Partners will describe some of the most significant effects of the building professions' adoption (or non-adoption) of CAD/CAM tools, including the resulting effects on contractual relationships among the various parties.

André Chaszar is the author of this article and editor of the 'Blurring the Lines' series in this year's volume of 3+. He is the founder of O-Design Consulting in New York, where he also teaches and conducts research in CAD/CAM applications to architecture. He is currently writing a book on cad/cam, for publication in 2004, for Wiley-Academy.

Below left
A winter roofscape at Dia:Beacon, the new museum of the Dia Foundation, displays snow-covered ducts positioned by the architects to avoid blocking roof monitor windows above the galleries.

Below right
Inside the museum, new white walls contrast with existing structural elements painted in a subtly different shade.

Architecture **Without** Architects

The current love affair between designers and visual artists started harmlessly enough and at first seemed like an innocent flirtation. Architects began fabricating art work for gallery exhibitions, and the line between the professions threatened to fade entirely. But then, in an unexpected reversal, artists started designing interiors. Here, **Craig Kellogg** examines two projects in New York that have recently been completed by artists. Should we, he wonders, fear this emerging trend?

Call Zaha Hadid a painter and Frank Gehry a sculptor; it's fair to say that both of them work outside the traditional bounds of design. Of course, neither Gehry nor Hadid has done much in New York. But you can't help noticing other crossover acts now surfacing in Manhattan. Take this spring's blockbuster museum exhibition of art projects by the firm Diller+Scofidio, at the Whitney Museum of American Art. I found myself hypnotised by the show's 'mural', which consisted of a robotic power-drill grinding the gallery walls into Swiss cheese. Call it form follows friction; the installation was as fraught and complex as the relationship between art and architecture has recently become.

While Diller+Scofidio's drill chewed through the walls of the art museum uptown, a counteroffensive was under way in New York's West Chelsea neighbourhood. For Balenciaga, the venerable French fashion house, an artist was transforming the ground floor of a former printing plant into a boutique. 'I didn't want to do something that was related to interiors,' said the artist,

Below left
Three rusted-steel ellipses by Richard Serra have been permanently installed in the old printing factory that now serves as a museum for the Dia Art Foundation in Beacon, New York.

Below, top right
Michael Heizer's ultra-minimalist installation at Dia:Beacon comprises steel-lined voids that puncture the floor and plunge through the cellar level.

Below, bottom right
A 1997 John Chamberlain sculpture occupies part of the former factory floor at Dia: Beacon, under sawtooth skylights facing north.

Dominique Gonzalez-Foerster, who received the 2002 Marcel Duchamp award. 'I'm not an architect.'

Working with Balenciaga's head designer Nicolas Ghesquière, Gonzalez-Foerster took landscape architecture as her metaphor for the new boutique. The clothes hang from lacquered metal racks that reinterpret mid-century garden arbours by the California landscape architect Garrett Eckbo. For the feeling of clouds moving overhead, a ceiling of chic, slim fluorescent tubes is wired to dim in slowly rolling patterns.

The project architect, who seems not to have been terribly necessary, was supplied by the contractor. 'He was very good in rocks,' Gonzalez-Foerster says. She was pleased with his source for the 'greenish-bluish' boulders set into a concrete ramp inside the front of the store. Scattered throughout the space are André Cazenave's artificial rocks illuminated by light bulbs from within.

The few new walls are faceted to evoke outcroppings – or icebergs. Otherwise, though, the shop seems barely renovated. Forget the minimal aesthetic; here the design process itself was minimalist. In terms of the finishes, an architect might have emphasised the structure more – and eliminated the industrial grime the printers left behind. But battered old columns, patched walls and spattered concrete floors remain unpainted. Because it is an interior renovation, the designers were not bound by annoying architectural concerns. No doubt there are architects who would hesitate to call the Balenciaga store architecture. Maybe it isn't, though it is a vest-pocket jewel.

At a more impossible scale – larger, in fact, than the galleries of New York's Whitney Museum of American Art, Guggenheim Museum and MoMA combined – is Dia Art Foundation's new freestanding museum in Beacon, New York. If not more influential, here the architects were at least more necessary because of the scope of work. Renovations at Dia were long and exhaustive. But despite extreme measures – the ripping up of floors and insertion of mechanical systems – the purity of the industrial architecture of

Below, top
At Balenciaga's new boutique in Manhattan, warm and cool fluorescent tubes are scattered above the selling floor.

Below, bottom
A desk for sales associates at the shop contrasts the naturalism of a formed boulder with a conspicuously man-made green plastic writing surface.

Below
Balenciaga garments are displayed on metal pergolas inspired by the Modernist landscape architecture of Garrett Eckbo.

the original factory with sawtooth skylights has been preserved. There are few fingerprints.

The foundation attributes the renovation to the famous artist Robert Irwin, in collaboration with the unknown architectural firm OpenOffice. I took the extra trouble of learning the firm principals' names. They are Lyn Rice and Galia Solomonoff.

Rice and Solomonoff apparently worked for Irwin. From hundreds of glass samples the architects found, he selected beautiful clear and translucent panes to reglaze the windows, in beguiling patterns that filter the view. They also made Irwin a 5-inch-tall museum dolls-house where scaled down replicas of art in Dia's collection were 'installed' to check for proper fit. So far so good. However, Irwin is also credited with the design of the museum's fire exits. I wonder how much time he spent sitting down with a calculator and the town's fire-code books.

Extensive new ventilation ducts run on the roof so that they will not be visible to gallery goers. In truth, the ducts probably don't belong on the roof at Dia. They are mounted atop metal stilts and had to be engineered to withstand snow loads. Although they have been heavily insulated, there must be some inevitable heat losses with this system. And I wonder about the zillion holes that were punched through the roof to deliver the air from the ducts. Leaks anyone?

You can argue that the design is functional because it serves the art, which is subtle and demands the barest of rooms unencumbered by ducts. Fortunately, at Dia, a lavish budget allowed endless fiddling with such elements, leaks be damned.

Even supervising their own designs, there's no question that architects sometimes get tangled in their systems and details. You could certainly argue that a more traditional design process, with an architect in charge, would have imposed limits and curbed artistic freedoms. But, on the other hand, when circumstances are less posh than at Dia:Beacon, architects can nudge logical design decisions in the direction of beauty. For the man who is not a prince and patron, that is function – the value and the duty of an architect – in a nutshell. ⊿

1 Houston: Downtown. In a bizarre reversal of urbanity, entire blocks have been razed to provide car parks. A few fragments of original buildings are shown in the middle distance.

2 Houston: Downtown. The decks of the car parks form an artificial landscape of ramps and steps. These private car-parks are connected to the private tunnel system that completely bypasses the street level.

3 Houston: Freedmanstown. These houses, seemingly straight out of a textbook by Aldo Rossi, were built for freed slaves after the American Civil War. Unlike the suburban ghettos of Los Angeles, they retain some gradation between the communal public realm and the private interior.

4 Houston: Southmore. Houses in the Museum District evoke a timeless picture of Americana. In contrast to the parodies of American 'New Urbanism', the Museum District includes mixed uses, incomes and races.

Urban Entropy: A Tale of Three Cities

Thomas Deckker presents a snapshot, illustrated with his own photographs, of some recent literature that focuses on the urban transformations that are taking place – most specifically in Los Angeles, Houston and London.

In the Park Central Hotel in downtown Fort Worth is an intriguing photograph. John Fitzgerald Kennedy spent the night of 21 November 1963 at the Hotel Texas there before continuing on to Dallas; the photograph shows him mobbed by supporters outside the hotel in his – fatally unprotected – limousine. When one turns and looks out the window the same street is unrecognisable. Instead of the dense blocks of offices, hotels and department stores is an open grid of car parks; only a few isolated buildings remain.

The transformation of American cities has been viewed as a natural phenomenon, as a 'survival of the fittest' – not least by its beneficiaries – and it is, perhaps, a surprise to find the quantity of opinion directed against this assumption. No city has been the subject of so much critical attention as Los Angeles, most famously, perhaps, by Edward W Soja, Frederic Jameson, Lynne Spigel and Mike Davis, to the point where it has become a metonym for disastrous urban development. Davis in particular has charted the future decline of Los Angeles through its own 'internal contradictions' by social division in *City of Quartz: Excavating the Future in Los Angeles* (1990), by courting natural disaster in *Ecology of Fear: Los Angeles and the Imagination of Disaster* (1998), and by the displacement of the Anglo population by the Hispanic in *Magical Urbanism* (2000). Finally, in *Dead Cities and Other Tales* (2002), Davis extends his metaphorical description of capitalism as war to American landscapes and cityscapes.

Davis's thesis in *Dead Cities* is how American capitalism – insane and unfettered greed, endemic racism against Hispanics, African-Americans and Native Americans, and the collusion of government, monopolistic industries and an unaccountable military – has brought not only Los Angeles but the whole Southwest to the brink of environmental disaster, not least because of the nuclear, chemical and biological development sites, and social adversity. The parallels Davis draws to the expansion and suburbanisation of Los Angeles that began during the Second World War are intriguing. He notes that, in 1942, the US Army was building (and rebuilding) full-size models of the centres of Berlin (advised by Erich Mendelsohn) and Tokyo (advised by Antonin Raymond) in Nevada to perfect the destruction of their civilian populations and urban cultures by aerial bombardment. I am sure we are all familiar with photographs of the results.

Few downtowns, however, could look as devastated as that of Houston. Houston is, in many respects, a more extreme but less glamorous version of Los Angeles. It stretches towards Galveston, much as London stretches towards Brighton, but with only two million inhabitants its density is one-quarter that of Los Angeles. Lars Lerup and Albert Pope, dean and professor respectively at Rice University, have both found a less apocalyptic critical voice for their city. Pope fully deserves to join Soja and Jameson; in *Ladders* he provides a precise analysis of how 20th-century suburbanisation developed along closed 'ladder' grids, that is, cul-de-sacs along freeways, rather than 19th-century open rectilinear grids. This new and parallel sub-urbanism could hardly be said to be a populist reaction to architectural theory: it was partly based on the English garden city ideal of Ebenezer Howard in the 1890s and Barry Parker and Raymond Unwin in the 1900s, and on its later development by Ludwig Hilbersheimer in the 1940s (Richard Neutra was also implicated). Pope, quoting the second law of thermodynamics, concludes that entropy, a condition of 'chaos and sameness' has replaced 'organisation and differentiation' as the paradigm of the urban condition.

How that entropic urban condition is articulated is described by Lerup in *After the City* (2000), an

5 London: Royal Albert Dock. The London docks were a major target for the Luftwaffe during the Second World War. By turning their attention from airfields and radar stations, the Luftwaffe, ironically, gave the almost-defeated RAF time to recover and ultimately repulse them.

6 London: Royal Albert Dock. Within 15 years of their attempted destruction by the Luftwaffe, the dock buildings would be redundant due to the universal adoption of the shipping container. Their present transformation has been to bizarre super-scaled canalside houses, a truly 'postmodern' falsification of history.

7 London: Royal Victoria Dock. The erasure of the buildings left a subtle landscape in which the history of the site is inscribed through railway lines, materials and changes in level.

8 London: Beckton Gasworks. Having survived the attentions of the Luftwaffe, this gasworks finally succumbed to Stanley Kubrick as Vietnam in his film *Full Metal Jacket*.

1

5

2

6

3

7

4

8

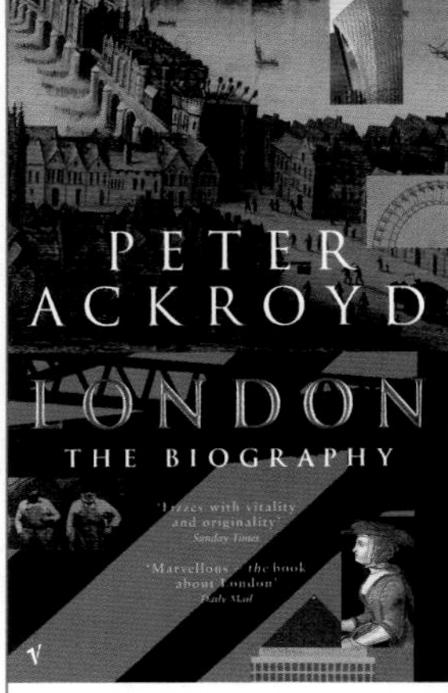

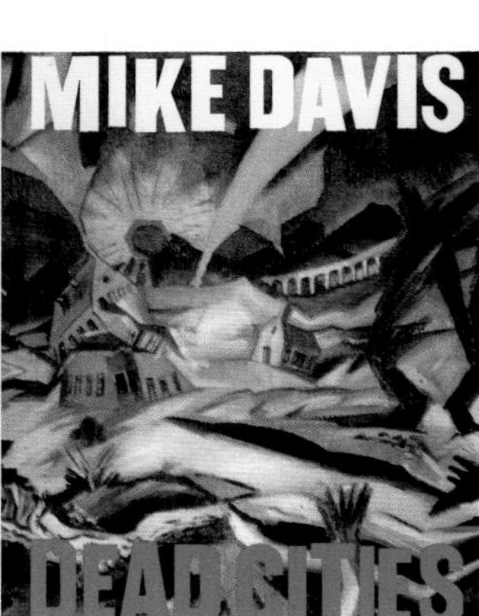

Urban Bibliography

Peter Ackroyd, *London: The Biography,* Vintage (London), 2001

Mike Davis, *City of Quartz: Excavating the Future in Los Angeles,* Verso (London and New York), 1990

Mike Davis, *Ecology of Fear: Los Angeles and the Imagination of Disaster,* Holt (New York), 1998

Mike Davis, *Magical Urbanism: Latinos Reinvent the US City,* Verso (London and New York), 2000

Mike Davis, *Dead Cities and Other Tales,* The New Press (New York), 2002

Lars Lerup, *After the City* , MIT Press (Cambridge, MA), 2000

Albert Pope, *Ladders,* Rice University School of Architecture and Princeton Architectural Press, 1996

Iain Sinclair, *London Orbital: A Walk Around the M25,* Granta Books (London and New York), 2002

enlargement of the thesis first published as 'Stim & Dross: Rethinking the Metropolis' in assemblage in 1994, that out of a 'zoomorphic field' of dross ('dregs'), occasional stims ('stimulations', or from the German *Stimme*, 'voice') occur that, borrowing an analogy from chaos theory, briefly act as 'strange attractors' for urban life. Such stims have no use for architecture: they are social rather than spatial. George O Jackson's photographs of freeways, vacant plots and parking revisit the territory of Robert Smithson and Ed Ruscha. Pope calls this the 'aesthetic of emptiness'.

However, no visitor to Houston, particularly if they are visiting Renzo Piano's Menil Collection, could fail to be impressed by the Museum District in which it is found. The Museum District is an area of mixed-use *par excellence*: middle-class homes, museums, Rice University itself, restaurants and shops, with a prosperous Hispanic district adjacent. This is the area that Lerup calls the 'middle landscape', an indeterminate zone inside the inner freeway loop, between downtown and suburbs, and squalor and growth. This middle landscape has developed without the formal architectural theories and corporate construction system of the suburbs, but rather through cooperative anarchy; it is an 'open' system of creation rather than the 'closed' system in which entropy is inevitable. It will be strangely familiar to the inhabitants of London.

If violence, turmoil, greed and ignorance are the factors Davis sees as ensuring the decline of American cities, they are exactly those that Peter Ackroyd believes have ensured London's rise to world prominence. From this viewpoint, the well-meaning but patronising Abercrombie plan seems surely a fleeting aberration in a Darwinian struggle. Darwin's thesis was, of course, not 'the survival of the fittest' popularly supposed by theoreticians of capitalism but survival through adaptation to changing environments. In *London - The Biography* (2001), Ackroyd charts the growth of what used to be known as the 'modern Babylon' and its decline after the Second World War, partly a result of it emptying into the garden cities and new towns beyond the green belt. The 'aesthetic of emptiness' governs London as much as Houston; if it necessarily needs its 'other', then it surely has created it along the M25, a bizarre world of insane asylums, military establishments and secretive corporations mapped out by Iain Sinclair in *London Orbital: A Walk Around the M25* (2002). Yet Ackroyd's final chapter is 'Resurgam'. The return of London to a kind of co-operative anarchy may be, instead of its decline, a sign of its survival in the late capitalist world. AD

Thomas Deckker is an architect in private practice in London. He teaches architecture and urban design in London and Switzerland.

Below
To pass through the chain-link security fence is to be transported in time to a Dickensian world of narrow cobblestone streets and grimy Victorian brick buildings. Even the signage for the aptly named Pumphouse Lane remains intact.

Gooderham and Worts Distillery

Toronto, Canada

Sean Stanwick describes how a 19th-century distillery in the centre of Toronto has become a major focus of urban regeneration.

With increasing frequency, brownfield developments are being viewed as an antidote to declining urban economies and suburban sprawl. A new project in the heart of Toronto, the most ambitious historic industrial renovation in its history, is poised to test this concept. To pass through the chain-link security fence of the Gooderham and Worts Distillery is to be transported back in time to a Dickensian world of narrow cobblestone streets and grimy Victorian brick buildings replete with the still-odorous relics of a long-forgotten era.

In 1831, Norfolk-born James Worts and brother-in-law William Gooderham set up a flour mill at the mouth of Toronto's Don River. When Gooderham realised that spirits were as staple as was food and shelter to the burgeoning community, he added a still in 1837. By Confederation, the distillery was producing over two million barrels of rye whiskey a year, and in as few as 10 years it was the largest distillery in the British Empire. Gradually the buildings fell silent, with only one

Below
The intricate facade of the pure spirits building was designed to give way in the event of an explosion, a frequent occurrence in the distilling process.

bottling line turning out amber rum until it, too, stopped production in 1990.

Of the 100 buildings that made up the original distillery, only 45 remain. Amidst the random collage of buildings that date to between 1860 and 1900, there is a cooperage, a pump house, stables, rack houses and barrel houses. Designed by the father-and-son team, both named David Roberts, the majority of the structures are of heavy timber, post-and-beam construction with brick or stone walls. And while they might be described as architecturally robust, a consistent stylish flourish and an industrial elegance are revealed in the brick friezes, stone corbelling and wooden fenestration. The stone distillery, built in the 1850s, is the oldest and most prominent building on the site. Built of pure-white limestone its architectural presence and clarity of form is highlighted by heavy corner coining and horizontal banding to articulate floor levels.

The buildings also bear direct witness to their utilitarian requirements. The pure spirits building of the 1870s, for example, frames an intricate glass facade with massive brick piers. Yet the aesthetic beauty of the fenestration belies its true function: in the event of an explosion, the facade was designed to give way leaving the building intact.

Interestingly, the buildings were constructed in a time when it made sense to produce everything needed on site, from the barrels to age the whiskey to the labels on the bottles. In fact, many of these original relics still dot the site. Antique steel-hoppers, wooden-wheeled factory carts, pulleys and corn mills sit silently under a veil of dust, disturbed only by film crews who have long known the site to be a prime movie location. Even the signage for the aptly named Pumphouse and Tankhouse Lanes remains in place.

While Victorian factories are quite common in the UK, a site of this size and condition is a true anomaly in Canada. Located a short 15-minute walk from the eastern edge of the downtown core, King and Parliament were once the epicentre of Toronto's vibrant industrial past. Today the area is defined by a rail corridor and a decaying raised motorway, and is for the most part an unloved and derelict swath of urban real estate.

Below
Sandra Ainsley Gallery. The exposed brick and industrial aesthetic of the cooperage provides a gritty backdrop for the organic glass sculptures of renowned American artist Dale Chihuly.

This, however, is about to change. After a successive chain of owners, including Hiram Walker in the 1920s, and most recently the pension fund of British-based wine and spirits company Allied Domecq, Cityscape Development Corporation purchased the project for $11 million in December 2002. With an eye on creating Toronto's first true pedestrian quarter, the site is set to morph into an arts and leisure community of resident artists and studios, cafés, galleries, restaurants and residential units. And while there have been many plans afoot over as many years to develop the land, it was Cityscape's community vision, and not the typical theme park approach, that finally took hold.

But as history has often shown, using artists as a catalyst for gentrification can often backfire as high-end retailers, attracted by the buzz of a creative neighbourhood, eventually drive the artists out. Knowing this, Cityscape has secured a 20-year lease deal with Artscape, a nonprofit organisation that finds permanent, affordable studio space for artists and performers.

That the site is now attracting so much attention seems well timed and in fact comes on the heels of other international reuse projects. Drawing parallels with the lively outdoor spaces of New York's SoHo or Vancouver's Granville Island, city planners are hoping that the precinct will serve as an important catalyst in the official plan to stimulate residential and commercial growth in the area, and of course keep the fire lit on their nascent waterfront-development plans.

While the 13-acre site was designated a national historic area in 1988, it has, however, brought to the fore the uneasy tension between conservation and development. According to John Berman, a partner in Cityscape: 'The corporate philosophy a decade ago was to tear these properties down and take the lands that they were built on.' Fortunately, Allied Domecq took its custodial responsibilities seriously and has left the project in an impeccable state of preservation. Michael McClelland of ERA Architects, the firm policing the architectural restoration, says: 'Our planning mandate is to adopt a sympathetic reuse policy. The trick is to convince tenants to leave the buildings as they are and take a light touch with minimal intervention.' To police the work, ERA has implemented a set of design guidelines that govern the overall architectural vision of the project while at the same time leaving individual tenants the freedom to renovate their own spaces as they see fit. This appears to be an amenable development strategy. With the site already 85 per cent occupied, ERA is currently overseeing the work of several noted architects including Shim Sutcliffe, and Kuwabara Payne McKenna Blumberg, who are renovating space for the Soulpepper Theater for George Brown College.

Working to meet the May 2003 opening, the site is abuzz with tradespeople restoring decayed windows, cleaning bricks and recycling timber reclaimed from floorboards or roof beams. While all 45 buildings will be restored in a rapid but phased development over the next two years, renovating the purpose-built factories will undoubtedly test the resourcefulness of its architects. Inside the sprouting building, the ceilings are only 2 metres high. The cask building presents a similar challenge; its 80-foot interior is a three-dimensional grid of rough-hewn lumber shelving where thousands of whiskey barrels once sat ageing, but as the racks are the building's structure, removal is impossible. Says McClelland: 'It's an exciting time, but it's also laced with poignancy, attended with a certain loss of innocence because these structures have remained uncorrupted and preserved for 150 years.'

Like Gooderham himself, the new tenants are seen as pioneers to the area. Early-comers include the Sandra Ainsley Gallery, the decorative art glass of which features the work of renowned artist Dale Chihuly and proves a perfect fit against the backdrop of the gritty cooperage. Other adventurers include Balzac's (a coffee house that is currently roasting its own beans in the pumphouse), Fluid Living Furniture and even a neighbourhood pub that has leased space.

As legend goes, workers were often paid in spirits rather than cash. Careful not to become too intoxicated by their own alacrity, Cityscape is hoping that the ghosts of those past, whose names are still etched in stone window ledges, will deliver a good omen to the project. In a most apropos move, organic spirits are once again flowing from the 6,000-square-foot Mill Street microbrewery. It seems likely, then, that the city will reap more than a financial reward, and can once again enjoy its founding spirits. AD

Based in Toronto, Sean Stanwick is a regular contributor to AD who has a particular interest in the urban and the themed spectacular. He has also contributed to *Sustaining Architecture in the Anti-Machine Age* (Wiley-Academy) and is currently co-writing *Winery Builders* and *Community Builders* (also for Wiley). He is an instructor with the Royal Architectural Institute of Canada and is currently a design architect with Farrow Partnership Architects in Toronto.

Subscribe Now

As an influential and prestigious architectural publication, *Architectural Design* has an almost unrivalled reputation worldwide. Published bimonthly, it successfully combines the currency and topicality of a newsstand journal with the editorial rigour and design qualities of a book. Consistently at the forefront of cultural thought and design since the 1960s, it has time and again proved provocative and inspirational – inspiring theoretical, creative and technological advances. Prominent in the 1980s for the part it played in Postmodernism and then in Deconstruction, AD has recently taken a pioneering role in the technological revolution of the 1990s. With groundbreaking titles dealing with cyberspace and hypersurface architecture, it has pursued the conceptual and critical implications of high-end computer software and virtual realities. AD

AD Architectural Design

SUBSCRIPTION RATES 2003
Institutional Rate: UK £160
Personal Rate: UK £99
Discount Student* Rate: UK £70
OUTSIDE UK
Institutional Rate: US $240
Personal Rate: US $150
Student* Rate: US $105

*Proof of studentship will be required when placing an order. Prices reflect rates for a 2002 subscription and are subject to change without notice.

TO SUBSCRIBE
Phone your credit card order:
+44 (0)1243 843 828

Fax your credit card order to:
+44 (0)1243 770 432

Email your credit card order to:
cs-journals@wiley.co.uk

Post your credit card or cheque order to:
John Wiley & Sons Ltd.
Journals Administration Department
1 Oldlands Way
Bognor Regis
West Sussex PO22 9SA
UK

Please include your postal delivery address with your order.

All AD volumes are available individually.
To place an order please write to:
John Wiley & Sons Ltd
Customer Services
1 Oldlands Way
Bognor Regis
West Sussex PO22 9SA

Please quote the ISBN number of the issue(s) you are ordering.

AD is available to purchase on both a subscription basis and as individual volumes

○ I wish to subscribe to AD *Architectural Design* at the **Institutional rate of £160**.

○ I wish to subscribe to AD *Architectural Design* at the **Personal rate of £99**.

○ I wish to subscribe to AD *Architectural Design* at the **Student rate of £70**.

○ AD *Architectural* Design is available to individuals on either a calendar year or rolling annual basis; Institutional subscriptions are only available on a calendar year basis. Tick this box if you would like your Personal or Student subscription on a rolling annual basis.

○ Payment enclosed by Cheque/Money order/Drafts.

Value/Currency £/US$ ______

○ Please charge £/US$ ______ to my credit card.

Account number:

Expiry date:

Card: Visa/Amex/Mastercard/Eurocard *(delete as applicable)*

Cardholder's signature

Cardholder's name

Address

Post/Zip Code

Recipient's name

Address

Post/Zip Code

I would like to buy the following issues at £22.50 each:

○ AD 165 *Urban Flashes Asia*, Nicholas Boyarsky + Peter Lang
○ AD 164 *Home Front: New Developments in Housing*, Lucy Bullivant
○ AD 163 *Art + Architecture*, Ivan Margolius
○ AD 162 *Surface Consciousness*, Mark Taylor
○ AD 161 *Off the Radar*, Brian Carter + Annette LeCuyer
○ AD 160 *Food + Architecture*, Karen A Franck
○ AD 159 *Versioning in Architecture*, SHoP
○ AD 158 *Furniture + Architecture*, Edwin Heathcote
○ AD 157 *Reflexive Architecture*, Neil Spiller
○ AD 156 *Poetics in Architecture*, Leon van Schaik
○ AD 155 *Contemporary Techniques in Architecture*, Ali Rahim
○ AD 154 *Fame and Architecture*, J. Chance and T. Schmiedeknecht
○ AD 153 *Looking Back in Envy*, Jan Kaplicky
○ AD 152 *Green Architecture*, Brian Edwards
○ AD 151 *New Babylonians*, Iain Borden + Sandy McCreery
○ AD 150 *Architecture + Animation*, Bob Fear
○ AD 149 *Young Blood*, Neil Spiller
○ AD 148 *Fashion and Architecture*, Martin Pawley
○ AD 147 *The Tragic in Architecture*, Richard Patterson
○ AD 146 *The Transformable House*, Jonathan Bell and Sally Godwin
○ AD 145 *Contemporary Processes in Architecture*, Ali Rahim
○ AD 144 *Space Architecture*, Dr Rachel Armstrong
○ AD 143 *Architecture and Film II*, Bob Fear
○ AD 142 *Millennium Architecture*, Maggie Toy and Charles Jencks
○ AD 141 *Hypersurface Architecture II*, Stephen Perrella
○ AD 140 *Architecture of the Borderlands*, Teddy Cruz